PENGUIN BOOKS
AWĀRA

Gayatri Chatterjee is an independent scholar working in film
and cultural studies. Based in Pune, she teaches in India and
has lectured widely in USA and Europe. *Awāra* was awarded
the Swarna Kamal, the President's Gold Medal, for the Best
Book on Cinema. She is also the author of *Mother India* (2002).

AWĀRA

GAYATRI CHATTERJEE

PENGUIN BOOKS

An imprint of Penguin Random House

PENGUIN BOOKS

Penguin Books is an imprint of the Penguin Random House group of companies
whose addresses can be found at global.penguinrandomhouse.com

Published by Penguin Random House India Pvt. Ltd
4th Floor, Capital Tower 1, MG Road,
Gurugram 122 002, Haryana, India

First published by Wiley Eastern Limited 1992
Published by Penguin Books India 2003
This edition published in Penguin Books by Penguin Random House India 2025

ISBN 9780143029809

Typeset in Sabon LT Std by Manipal Technologies Limited, Manipal
Printed at Replika Press Pvt. Ltd, India

www.penguin.co.in

MIX
Paper | Supporting
responsible forestry
FSC™ C016779

To Bill
(William Rothman)

CONTENTS

AWĀRA

(The Vagabond) B&W, 170 mins

Language: Hindustani
Direction: Raj Kapoor
Story: K.A. Abbas, V.P. Sathe
Screenplay & Dialogue: K.A. Abbas
Camera: Radhu Karmakar
Editing: G.G. Mayekar
Art Direction: M.R. Achrekar
Sound: Allauddin
Lyrics: Hasrat Jaipuri, Shailendra
Music: Shanker, Jaikishen
Playback: Shamshad Begum, Lata Mangeshkar,
     Mukesh, Mohammad Rafi, Manna Dey
Cast: Prithviraj Kapoor, Nargis, Raj Kapoor,
     K.N. Singh, Leela Chitnis, Shashiraj, Cuckoo,
     Zubeida, Shashi Kapoor, Honey O'Brian,
     Leela Misra

Production: R.K. Films
Released at: Royal Opera House, Bombay
Released on: 21 December 1951

PREFACE TO THE SECOND EDITION

When Penguin told me of their decision to reissue *Awāra*, I was delighted. The old book would see the light of the day again! I also felt humbled. Just a few months ago, Penguin had brought out an edition of my second book, *Mother India,* putting it within easy reach of an Indian readership. I thought I had made good progress and written the second book better than the first, but now I was getting to hear things like, 'I like your second book, but I like the first one better. In *Awāra*, we are always close to the film. *Mother India* does have much more information, but then the pleasure of reading about a film is interrupted and we must think of other things.' It was interesting to learn through such experiences that books undertaken with a particular purpose or logic at the time of writing continue to make sense in different ways years after their first appearance. Penguin's decision to reissue *Awāra,* eleven years after its original publication, made me reconsider what I had tried to do then and assess the book's position in the history of film studies in India. Eventually, I decided to let the text be reprinted without any changes, and only add a new preface.

I have also been working for some time on a book-length study of another film, Damle and Fattelal's 1935 Marathi devotional *Sant Tukaram*. In the course of writing these one-film monographs, I have become accustomed to people in India expressing surprise: 'A whole book about just one film!' The clear aim before me when I wrote *Awāra* was to energize the field of film studies around Indian films, to encourage people to go in for repeated viewings of films, and to devote more thought to each film they saw than has been customary. While teaching film to students from all over the country, my experience has been that the exercise of going through a film in the classroom—following its visual and narrative construction, decoding it, going over the cultural or political references—meets with enthusiastic participation. But when it comes to books and articles, the general expectation has been that critical writings must *scold*. A serious writer was supposed to denounce a film—particularly one belonging to the mainstream. The problem was linked to confusions about the status of 'art film' and 'commercial film' and there was at one time much talk directed at correcting the situation. There is no art film or commercial film—a film is either *good* or *bad*. What has been hard to get rid of is this judgmental tendency—a serious book is meant to satisfy these tendencies and to place things in bipolar opposition.

But the problem does not end here. A related expectation is that if one was serious, one could appreciate films of Satyajit Ray or Ritwik Ghatak, for example. No doubt, all such muddles stem from serious concerns—a stage of confusion marks the initial lack of adequate thinking and writing on questions that themselves have real urgency and substance. This is one reason why the history of our efforts at film studies in this country is so interesting and needs to be chronicled. My endeavour towards clarity, at the time of writing *Awāra,* was to engage in close studies of individual films and situate films and their study in the various histories of the country.

One obvious corrective that has grown over recent years is the demand to know more about Indian commercial films—recent ones, as well as films of the studio years. The contemporary mood seems to be declaring: We *are* talking about films and we feel no shame as *cinéphiles*. And it is now all right to discuss popular cinema. Increasingly, readers are taking to the pleasures of getting close to a film—the pleasure there is in the repeated viewing of a film, reading about a film one has liked once, in finding things that had escaped one's notice on first viewing or seeing it in different lights. But the delay has not been good for Indian film studies.

In preparation for writing *Mother India,* I read several titles in the group of monographs to which the project ultimately belonged, the British Film Institute's

(BFI) Film Classics series.* In investigating how other authors had articulated themselves, I thought about the policies that enabled the publication of such a diverse concert of voices under one rubric. The BFI books have been appreciated throughout the world; the curator of the Harvard Film Archive, Bruce Jenkins, wrote of them in a private communication, 'These books have set a gold standard for us in the world of film studies.' To pursue these is to see that one-film books can be written with passion and personal engagement, with results not necessarily to be confined to simple categories of *praise* or *abuse*.

A book on a film must show why the writer has found the film interesting; and the entire book must be filled up with stuff that others too will find interesting. And this actually has little to do with what is usually perceived as *liking*. After the publication of *Mother India,* a television interviewer asked me, 'So is this your favourite film?' to which I replied, 'If I am exiled alone on an island with ten films, this film will not feature on the list.' But if I am asked to write another monograph on *Mother India,* I would. There is much I haven't been able to put down and enough left from what I have written (because of the word limit) to yield another book. One does not teach a film or write about it only because one loves it.

---

* The British Film Institute launched the Film Classics series in 1992, bringing out five to six titles every year. *Mother India* was the sixty-sixth book.

The origins of *Awāra* date to December 1989, when Asang Machway of Wiley Eastern approached me for a series of three monographs. It was he who proposed *Awāra* as the first title. The suggestion had actually come after he had requested me to write 'a book on Indian Cinema'. 'What does that actually mean?' I had wondered aloud. We had discussed the issues involved and he was certain he did not want a historiography of Indian films. Nor did he want a discussion of a particular formal or sociological aspect. 'Can you write on one film, then?'

I was so happy! Maybe after one has gone through such exercises one gets ready to eventually write about all of Indian cinema—so I had thought. As much as anything, it was the novelty of the format and concept that made me accept his suggestion, for there were very few one-film books then (BFI had not yet launched the Film Classics series). Moreover, I sensed an increasing demand in classrooms all over for more input on Indian mainstream cinema, as opposed to the foreign films and works by a select body of Indian independent filmmakers that constituted the usual fare in film appreciation courses. I can say I have learnt about writing on cinema by teaching it. One outstanding feature of the original Film Appreciation Course, as designed by Satish Bahadur and P.K. Nair in Pune and organized jointly by the National Film Archive of India and the Film and Television Institute of India, had been selecting single films for teaching.

And that is how I have been trained. I had become accustomed to spending years over the study of a film, watching it repeatedly—I could not teach a film in the classroom unless I had seen it the previous day. And when subtitling work became part of my professional life, there too I learnt to spend time over the material of one film: image, sound, script.

So, when I wrote *Awāra*, I was extending my experiences of learning and teaching cinema. While I was clear about the problems and discussed those constantly with many colleagues, I was far from any definite answers. I was so acutely aware of what I had not been able to accomplish and what I was expected to!

There are twelve chapters in the book and they all open up to particular areas of film viewing, talking, studying and writing. The chapters are not well connected; in fact they do not flow one into the other. Many could thus say the book, in that way, is not at all *well structured*.

The first chapter begins at the beginning: the title of the film, the credit titles and the names of the principal protagonists. The attempt is to show how thematic and discursive concerns might permeate every aspect of a film and be discernible from the first image—even if it bears the credit titles. The second chapter is more ambitious in that it initiates the method of close *analysis* to demonstrate the filmmaker's cinematic awareness. Titled *The Father, and the Other Generations*, the chapter also identifies the historical foundations upon which the narration is woven and illustrates the various interrelationships between characters created out of a nationalist background. All this is delineated through mise en scène and editing. But the next chapter, Chapter 3, deviates from the structuralist methods previously adopted and essays to combine semiotics and feminist criticism, the representation of the woman in the films operates at different levels and serves to fulfil various narrative and ideological functions. The next two chapters draw upon other sources, literary mostly, to trace influences not only for this film but also of films that could be grouped together under a generic label. And thereby I align myself with the important question of the *genre* as posed vis-à-vis Indian cinema, by scholars like Ashish Rajadhyaksha and Ravi Vasudevan. But lacking confidence in the areas of Reception Theory (something other scholars were initiating at this period), I only question the *popular* in the sixth chapter. The seventh is a close look at one particular sequence/song picturization and elaboration of the theme. I have been fascinated by the obsessive representation of incestuous relationships in films both Indian and foreign, and propose further study and research; the chapter that follows is offered in part as an introduction to this problematic. Since that topic here is connected with the colonial and nationalist history of India, I club the two issues to call the chapter *Pursuits of Whiteness and Riches*. The tenth chapter isolates a particular item among the props used in the film—the childhood photograph of Rita. Through repeated use, it acquires tremendous significance, ultimately undermining and changing the *meanings* the character and its representation seemingly generate. Chapters 11 and 12 throw light on two distinctive and complementary aspects of Indian cinema—song and dance picturization and narrative structure. I end with a triptych: the director, the character and the actor— all present in and presented by Raj Kapoor. Kapoor was also the producer of the film; but that role and the financial/production aspects behind the film are missing entirely from my study. This is a lack I was to make up in my second book.

While I prepared to write *Mother India,* my editor at BFI, Rob White, suggested that I describe scenes and sequences in order to bring the film alive in such a way that the readers would go back to the film and view it again. In my turn, I informed him, since this was the first Indian title of that series, my treatment would not isolate any one particular aspect of the film and its history but would interlace description of shots; and sequences, history of production and reception and, along with a judicious dose of analysis and theory, the book would be a *véni* or a plait of several things.

When I wrote *Awāra,* I, of course, had no such definite ideas of how the book must be structured. Now I would like to describe the two books in the following fashion: *Awāra* is made like a film with very definite segmentations—the chapters. It is like a montage film with different montage principles guiding shots and their juxtapositions. *Mother India,* on the other hand, flows like a film that uses shots of long duration, where a few key preoccupations wind their way throughout.

At the time of its release, *Awāra* was panned by many critics for containing only textual analysis—a pejorative term with some scholars then. I have had people walking out of my class on finding I was engaged in *mere textual analysis*. On re-reading the book and examining my preferences today, what I find is that I have become interested in situating a filmic text in the context of the history of its time—the social, political and cultural. We need to think all over again what we would like to do with 'film text', and we need to do this against the background of the particular trajectory— or trajectories—of western film scholarship.

Going over the first preface, I find I do indicate 'questions that I seek to answer in the course of this book'. But the attempt is weak. What comes out loud and clear is my intention of not engaging with feminist criticism—not until I find out what Freud and Lacan mean in the Indian context. Now, I do indicate that Raj (Raj Kapoor) is the voyeur and Rita (Nargis) the object of his *look*. I could have dwelt on that aspect and made a firm connection with feminist criticism on the gendered *look*. But I was more interested in the relationship between Rita and Raghunath (Prithviraj Kapoor)—a relationship that led me to another different problematic: that of money and India's historical transition from feudalism to capitalism. It would have been useful to pursue an analysis of women's position under these two systems, but I do not think I was ready then for proposing far-reaching conclusions. What emerges is a suggestion that unless we have established a discussion of Indian economic and social history vis-a-vis India and the films we have made, the feminist criticism we practice will not have matured—for any patriarchal system that such a feminism interrogates, far from being monolithic or essential, rests on historical contingencies.

It is also, given this background, that I had declared that I was not engaging in feminist criticism initiated by Laura Mulvey. Her terms are not absent from my book—one still of Raj Kapoor is captioned 'The *look* that seeks pleasure' and the following one of Nargis, 'The object of pleasure'. But I have tried to move on to show that scopophilia is produced not only in the depiction of a *female object* but also in the case of a male. The stills from the musical sequence *'Hum tumse mohabbat karke sanam'* can be taken as an illustration of how a mainstream film creates audience pleasure through the representation of a male hero. If both the hero and the heroine in films are ultimately objects of pleasure, melodrama, etc., then we need to go slow and observe what *differences* there are in the two. A comprehensive study would be of value to film studies in general.

Earlier I remarked that the task of learning what Freudian psychoanalysis means in the Indian context is still before us; on the other hand, I also show *Awāra* as an Oedipal drama. Freudian ideas became popular in India in the wartime years, featuring widely in literature and casual discourses of the time. But the implications of Freudian principles for aspects of Indian life such as the joint family system, the relations of disciples to their gurus, or the distinctive attachments that bind children (especially male children) and their mothers— these await sustained scholarly attention. For example, there are often several fathers or mothers in the life of an individual. Gods and gurus are addressed both as father and mother—indeed, occasionally as both at the same time. The emergence of the modern individual, in the context of a pluralistic society with multilevel hierarchies, multiple attachments and processes of socialization, is a topic that will reward further inquiry.

In *Awāra,* Raj has two fathers, equally bad or good. This is a scheme that replicates western binaries. In the case of Rita, on the other hand, the biological father is of no consequence and the mother is entirely absent. Her relationship with Raj's father, with its suggestion of incest, gets to be a loaded question (yet more so when the above-mentioned factor of money is taken into account). Another distinctive element is the undercurrent of violence that pervades the relationship between the hero and the heroine. Such themes in *Awāra* are prominent markers within a broader psycho-social history—the development of a cinematic tradition remarkable for the widespread depiction of incestuous relationships, the near-obsessive representation of the 'inability to love', and so on—and it is such troubled nodes as these that will prove most revealing to an understanding of Indian cinema within the field of film studies (at least, that is what I believe).

On a related note, what I have called *male melodrama* is very important in Indian films—surely more than what we see in the west—and is something that needs to be evaluated before we can make statements about melodrama and the figure of the woman. Feminist criticism has demonstrated that the figure of the woman is always a means of signification for the male discourse in films made by male directors (although I should note that I have found astounding representations and verbalizations of women's questions in the works of some, admittedly a few, male film-makers). In mainstream films, *she* signifies *his* desire and frustration, joy and sorrow, aspiration and failure. It is always about the man and not about the woman—it cannot be. And if we do not study the history of masculinity, its construct and its representation, then we cannot understand the representation of women. We seem to know this latter history better and perhaps that in fact constitutes the problem. It is in this context that I say I am not ready for feminist criticism. 'What is Man' is the question raised by novels, to follow George Lucas and I feel, many films in India ask the same question. In Indian cinema, the question is not primarily a philosophical one, although certain habits of thoughts derived from popular philosophy may be behind some of the films' themes and dialogues. Rather, I would locate the question of problematic manhood in the historical and contemporary conditions of postcolonial modernity. I did not then (and I do not now) have the scope to engage this issue on a broader canvas.

My purpose in *Awāra* is to present issues and avenues that would inform better study of Indian cinema.* I hope *Awāra* will prove to be useful in that direction. I thank Ravi Singh and Penguin for their decision to bring out this and some other one-film monographs. We have need for some more.

---

*The big addition in *Mother India* was material regarding the production history of the film. *Awāra* had none of that—it has zero primary research behind it. New in the field, I felt intimidated visiting studios and actors; I had only met the cameraman, Radhu Karmakar, the scriptwriter, V.P. Sathe and (only once) the lyricist, Hasrat Jaipuri.

PREFACE TO THE FIRST EDITION

The questions that I seek to answer in the course of this book are drawn from conversations that opened up in the film appreciation classes in different parts of the country where I was working with *Awāra*. I assumed some of those questions or problems as given condition for my book. I took it for granted that popular cinema is held under suspicion for being 'unrealistic' at a time when most people almost swear by 'realism' as a principal requisite for art, forms of expression and communication. While this might not be the case for painting or poetry, for cinema and to an extent for literature too, there is some kind of an obsession with 'realism'. Now, without going into any exploration of the genesis of this need in the 'average Indian mind', without even stating my own classroom experiences that make me think that 'realism' can be seen as a major hurdle before any film thinking, I had to proceed to answer a set of questions thrown up by one particular film.

Realism is one of the issues that the book is negotiating with. For those who would like me to give my position on this issue here, I would say that every medium, every art form, every age—this last is important, and I repeat—every age has its own tryst, its own way of relating with Reality. One important reason for choosing *Awāra* has been the fact that this film surprisingly shows conspicuous signs of wanting to come to some one way of doing this—the film adopts many styles, which could have been only so many signs of confusion, but which is not there actually, since the instances of the use of the many 'styles' are quite precise.

Thus the book keeps shifting between discussing the film, discussing (or touching upon) certain established modes of thinking or film theories, and trying to establish a more definitive mode of discussing Indian cinema. As a result I might be disappointing both the categories of potential readers—if there exists such a precise divide, i.e., the lay and the academic. I have left many things half-said, many topics are not touched upon at all, while I have dwelt at length on certain details, thus upsetting the balance of the book. Though I feel pained and annoyed with myself when I read the book again and want to re-work several parts, I have let it go as it is: let the work be amorphous for some more time, till more concrete thinking emerges out of a larger (this work, together with all existing and future works on our popular cinema) body of thoughtful work. At this moment, we must realize and admit that not enough has been thought or written.

One topic that I have left untouched, however, is the current Feminist criticism, that had been sparked off in 1976 by a seminal article by Laura Mulvey. Today, Hollywood cinema is being re-read under the influence of her work and a growing body of work that has followed her essay, giving rise to modern Feminist criticism. Naturally, it was not possible, in the book, to state my reasons. I have often felt the need to strike up a dialogue with it, take off from some of its tenets or views—at times I *have* done that without spelling it out. One reason that I can give here is that I believe, together with some others, that some more work has to be underway before we can combine our thoughts with those. There has been some work by Indian scholars working abroad, who have approached the entire question of Indian mainstream cinema through the works of Mulvey and others. We have had problems with that—all this demands more prior work and discussions.

Similarly, some scholars have looked at Indian popular cinema as an extension of the *Natyashāstra* (the thoughts on *rasa* only and not the entire work). We require to do a much more exhaustive study of the *Rasashāstras,* of the Indian aesthetic theories; we need to link modern thinking with the traditional concepts of 'performance', the question of 'frontality', 'narrativity' with the more traditional ways of dealing with time and space, etc. As a matter of fact, film thinkers here require to be more in touch with other thinkers in other areas.

Laura Mulvey's theories are based upon Lacan's work on psychoanalysis. Psychoanalytical thinking must be more integrated into our thoughts, before we can make Mulvey's work the base of fresh work in our own areas. The question of an 'Indian' concept of the Self, of desire, of the 'gaze', of the business of 'seeing' (of *darshan*), etc., are the other prerequisites before us. What goes as feminist criticism in the country is the study of 'stereotypes'. I have my doubts about the supposed priority of the study of stereotypes which is an extension of the structuralism of the fifties. In many ways we might still be thinking in the manner the structuralists did (there are marks of that in my book), while the entire body of women's study today has moved far beyond it.

Another approach I have left untouched is implicit in Laura Mulvey's perceptive warning:

'It has been suggested that the interest of Hollywood 50s melodrama lies primarily in the way that fissures and contradictions can be shown, by means of textual analysis, to be undermining the film's ideological coherence, contradictions of a kind, whether on the level of form or of narrative incident, that seem to save the film from belonging blindly to the bourgeois ideology which produced them.

This argument depends on the premise that the project of this ideology is to conjure up a coherent picture of a world by concealing the incoherence caused by exploitation and oppression. In this view a text which defies unity and closure is quite clearly progressive. Although this line of argument has been productive and revealing, there is a way in which it has been trapped in a kind of Chinese box quite characteristic of melodrama itself. Ideological contradiction is the overt mainspring and specific content of melodrama, not a hidden, unconscious thread to be picked up only by special critical processes.' ('Notes on Sirk and Melodrama', in Christine Gledhill, (ed.), *Home is Where the Heart is,* BFI, London 1987, p. 75.)

We must also begin to talk about the way masculinity and femininity is perceived and constructed in India. In fact, a very natural reaction to this insistence upon an 'Indian thinking' is that firstly it can be dangerous and misleading and secondly, there lurks a narrow spirit of nationalism behind it all. One tends to ask, of course, 'Is there today anything truly or exclusively Indian'? One is only too familiar with the debates raging today, all much too vast and complex and demanding volumes of work. Keeping all this in mind, my defence at this point is that I do not suffer from any excessive nationalistic fervour. The 'Indian thinking' or the 'Indian way' cannot be ignored for many reasons—not all of them are clear to us yet. Every time a Western mind adds the phrase, at the end of a new presentation, 'in Western philosophy' or 'in the Western system', I sincerely believe that it is inviting other systems to join in the discussion. What is our hesitation to add 'in the Indian system'? If it is the lack of disciplined thinking in this modern time— we could remedy that. There is no doubt in our minds that there is plenty here that can be seen as alternative ways of looking at things (or very simply, altogether new ways), at certain areas of human thought and endeavour. We do not have any doubts in our minds that though a colonized and developing country, we have not lost our voice, that we have written our history with our 'language' and 'voice', that it is time also to ignore somewhat these historical conditions and embark upon some ahistorical thinking from time to time. Though all this lies way beyond my ken, I must situate myself in the midst of this debate humbly, acknowledging my inabilities, because *nanyah panthan vidyaté ayanaya*—there is no other way but this.

ACKNOWLEDGEMENTS

I am deeply grateful to P.K. Nair, without whose constant support much of what I am doing would not probably have been possible. I thank Vlada Petric, who was the first to be interested in my film thinking and encourage me in my activities. I thank Probal Dasgupta, who was present in those early days, clearing up confusions and untangling knots.

I am grateful to Bhaskar Chandavarkar, without whose guidance the chapter on music would not have taken shape. I am grateful to Radhu Karmakar and V.P. Sathe, who have given me valuable insights into the making of *Awāra*. I am particularly grateful to K.P.R. Nair for going through the arduous task of reproducing stills from a dupe print of the film and to A. John of the National Film Archive of India, for giving up his valuable off-duty hours so that the work on the stills could be possible. Warm thanks to Mini Srinivasan and T. Muralidharan for going through the shockingly messy early drafts of the book and providing me with the confidence I so needed at that stage.

And last but not the least, I am extremely grateful to Randhir Kapoor for generously giving permission to reproduce the photographs in the book.

THE TITLE OF THE FILM: THE NAMING OF CHARACTERS

Raj Kapoor's *Awāra,* as the name suggests, and as the fame goes, is the story of a vagabond, a tramp. He calls himself an awāra but ends up doing a lot of things for which one can hardly call him that. We see him as a tramp, singing on the roads—for a brief while; otherwise he is a thief, a social climber, a passionate lover, a murderer. We could say that he would like to be an awāra for it is not a bad word for him, but he would also like to shine bright as a star; yet we often see him in lights other than those inner ones that make a man 'a star of the skies'. Awārapan or 'trampness' is not a modus vivendi for him; in other words, he does not actually live on the roads, or roam around from village to village, town to town. But he can be considered a wanderer in a different sense. He is a wanderer because he does not feel at home anywhere; his natural habitat is not naturally his own. He does not belong to any society or any particular class of

1

society or maybe he belongs equally to all. Whether in a slum or in a palace, he is restless to leave. Perhaps he is destined to move, to orbit around; he sings, 'I am forever displaced by destiny, I am a star of the skies.' Maybe in that sense he is an awāra. This is what we will be looking into.

The star is beyond this world of ours. As a star, he rejects the world, the bit where he is. After all, one's own world can be the entire world at times. His world seems hellish to him. He sings, 'I do not want this hell: I want flowers, songs, love and spring,' things that are not to be found where he is, and so he is an awāra. But whether he actually, physically or mentally, embarks on this search is another matter we will be looking into. Our hero is a 'star' of another kind; the audience knows it too. But whether he is the kind of star that he is talking about, that he would like to be, is something to be investigated.

Yes, he does not leave, at least we do not see him leaving any place on his own accord. In fact he wants to settle down. He wants love; when he finds it, he wants to live with it. Once it is established that he is a thief, we see him happily settled in his 'profession'; he sings while at it. He knows what he is or what he does, and sings or jokes about it. He tells the heroine, 'I am a thief,' and describes his various activities, knowing that she will not believe it, told that way. But we know that he is telling the truth. His mother had defined the word for him and it had meant a waster, a hoodlum, a thief. So our hero turns into a thief and celebrates that fact, and the film is about a thief. And as the audience we have been loving this film, so he is 'a lovable thief'. What does all this mean? He is also spelling out another kind of truth, that as a star he steals the hearts of millions, just as he steals the heart of the girl in the film. Words like 'stealing' and 'heart' provide a rhetoric to the film. He steals hearts, and again when he is tried for social crimes in a social court, an appeal is made to someone's 'court of the heart'.

So he is a wanderer who wants to love: but what does he love more? His 'road' or his 'woman'? But a man who wants to love, wants love, songs, etc., is also one who commits murders. Thus, during the course of the film questions are thrown up about many words and many ideas. Many ambivalent attitudes and thoughts are manifested. There is an ambivalence about the name of the film itself. Either the director considers his protagonist an awāra and so the name matches the character; or it is a mockery and the name is not supposed to fit the man, and the mockery carries a suggestion of something other than his 'roadness' or his loving heart.

At the end of the film we see him seeking to settle down in yet another sense. He wants to be part of the establishment, the bureaucratic machinery that he has criticized so strongly just a while ago. He wants to be a lawyer, a judge, like the one he has been conflicting with, like his father, who is a judge. This time he wants

to live in a manner more acceptable to society. The
film ends with a promise that he will give up his ways,
his awārapan. So often *he is what he is not; or he is
not what he is.*[1] So we must find out whether he is an
awāra or not. So what we get is a story of a conflict.
Whether to conform or not to conform. But the words
and the visuals of the film lead to the end of all conflicts
and the promise of a compromise. He says, 'I will
come out and study and then become a lawyer, then
a judge and then a magistrate.' The prison gate closes
on him; he is imprisoned, he acquires an antithesis of
his 'roadness'. That is the last shot of the film. The
first shot of the film—seeing things in reverse—is of
the Bombay High Court. In the next shot we are inside
it. A few shots later the handcuffed hero is led into the
court and made to sit inside a fenced-off area. From
one structure to another, from one confinement to
another—in between a little bit of the road, the story
of the time when he was free, the story of his various
struggles, his life and his love, his crimes.

   This is the third film made by Raj Kapoor, after
Aag and *Barsaat*—'Fire' and 'Rain'. In this third film
he chooses a name that has a human element to it. He
asks K.A. Abbas to write the script,[2] for Abbas has
been making humane progressive films with 'socialistic'
themes. If the naming of the film was done with care,
then how much of social, political or philosophical
intentions had gone into the film and the name that
represents the film? Let us look at the name again.

The word awāra can have a social significance. An awāra is a person who is not bound by the ways of the society. He is normally poor, he has no money and does not care for it. Sheer poverty puts him outside the pale of interests of society. He does not like to work; he does not take part in any system of production. Even if he does work, it is for a short period of time: he can quit any time, keeping the choice of work to himself alone. He can be engaged in any kind of activity ranging from idle games, gambling to petty acts of lawlessness. This apathy to the social ways comes naturally to him. Even the law does not bother about him, leaving him to his own devices. This shows areas where the control of the legal system blurs, and does not necessarily posit any weakness or corruption within the law. Such a man can be a product of the ills of a society, or a type found in all societies at all times. Such characters abound in nineteenth and early twentieth century literature, e.g., in Dickens and Gorky; as well as in the tradition of vagabonds, itinerant minstrels and other kinds of roving men as described in the northern epics and medieval romances of the West and the dervish traditions of the East. This is a type common also in the Hollywood cinema, where the vagabond provides a view of life contradictory to that of the hero who is motivated to accomplish something, has a goal to achieve.

The name can have a *philosophical* connotation: an awāra is a person eager to find God or experience godness, and hence cannot be bothered with the demands of society. But he is not a religious person, though he is eager in a desperate way for 'union with God', and is out in search of his god, often embarking on a metaphoric physical journey. His ways seem outlandish and crazy and he sometimes goes against the rules and regulations of his society.

A third implication is that the man is smitten with love and is completely under its control: '*Awāra, pyaar ka mara*' (an awāra is done for, because of love). Either he is looking for love, or is in love with love itself. Maybe, he has already experienced it, but the love object does not belong to him. His passions and the desire to unite destroy his reasoning, his common sense and the sense of social decorum. In several living traditions, earthly and godly love approximate each other or collapse on top of each other. As the earthly love soars to transcendental heights, the loved one turns into a god or a goddess. On the other hand, the god is given a human form to facilitate the act of loving, and s/he comes down on the earth to engage in various plays with man.

The word awāra (and its equivalents) thus belongs to various philosophical systems, literary traditions and past or present modes of living. It is a name that raises resonances that cannot be denied, but whether the director and the scriptwriter had chosen the name carefully and consciously relating it to the film can only come out of the discussion that follows.

We begin with the naming itself, for if the film has a name then it must have some relevance for the film; it must be related to the film. The name however may have no connection with the film at all, for popular cinema does not allegedly put in much thinking into the naming of a film. In fact, one possible reason for the name has already been given. Raj Kapoor admired Charlie Chaplin; so he named his third film after The Great Tramp.[3]

The study begins with the premise that whatever we identify in a film as related to other things in the film itself, or to the totality of the film, or to the tradition of filmmaking, we consider as some kind of choice from several possible alternatives, and hence it deserves our attention. Once this premise is accepted, the appearance of something apparently insignificant comes to be questioned at once. With that in mind, we can take up a study of the naming of the characters in *Awāra,* for the names, as we shall see, were chosen with care.

The Naming of Characters

The hero of the film is called Raj. Here is an example of how chance, design and happy accidents go to make successful films. The maker of the film lent his own name to his protagonist;[4] and Kapoor proved to be quite lucky. His name suggests something that is the very opposite of a tramp, a homeless moneyless vagabond, ridiculed or despised by everyone. He is the king, the superman in possession of material and supposedly physical and intellectual wealth.

If we can set aside the ideological problem that might arise here with the use of a name that means 'a king', then will we be able to see what is of interest here. Behind the use of this name which is antithetical to the concept implicit in the title of the film and the name of its hero, there can be the following reasons (as well as effects):

1. That of irony and pathos; the sad end of a man called Raj can increase the irony and the pathos in the drama.
2. Identification and intimacy with the character as well as the actor (and the director).

The second is clearly intended by the director. The director lends his name to the character, for the audience will see him in the character and love both. There is yet another instance of Kapoor's awareness of the fact that the star Raj Kapoor is acting as the hero Raj and that it has a special meaning for the film. In the very beginning of the film, before the entrance of any of the characters of the story, two journalists appear chatting. One of them says at some point, 'Look, your pal is coming.' The shot cuts to the entry of Raj Kapoor. These two characters, who are not a part of the narrative, carry out two functions:

1. Firstly, they are made to follow the tradition of 'announcing' characters.
2. Secondly, they underscore the audience's 'recognition' of their favourite star.

A couple of shots earlier Prithviraj Kapoor had made his entry into the courtroom and in the film. The audience had, without any doubt, recognized the thespian. But then the words heralding him had been, 'Here comes Justice Raghunath.'

Since this film was not concerned with the audience's recognition of this actor at that point there was no underlining gesture appearing in the film. But for the actor Raj Kapoor the director Raj Kapoor puts in a sentence, or rather a 'gag' that is a common practice for emphasizing the entry of a character. The audience knows these tricks or 'gags' of the popular cinema. Thus, a dynamic relationship gets established between a film and the filmic experience.

Rarely does the popular cinema audience remember a director while viewing a film (most of the time they do not even know the name of the director). But one is always aware of the actor behind the main character. Even if initially one comes with the preparation to see a Bimal Roy or a Manmohan Desai film, eventually it is only Dilip Kumar or Amitabh Bachchan one is conscious of. In *Awāra*, the personalities of the actor and the director, though they are one, collapse on the character, for here all three are one. As a result, the

identification with the character shifts between the
actor and the director. For example, whenever Raj
says, 'No fault of yours/his/hers with the way my face
is!' (explaining away the misunderstandings that come
his way), one knows that the sentence comes from the
actor Raj Kapoor, talking of his actor's face. When
Raj criticizes the house of Raghunath, 'A judge, and
he has such a big house!' the criticism is coming from
the director. It is he who has used such a big and posh
set and then has put these words into the mouth of the
hero, to run down the very use. But the sentence, 'No
fault of yours/his/hers, with the way my face is', brings
us round to laugh at Raj, sympathize with him, fall in
love with him. And all the while we are also conscious
that the actor himself is talking there.

Thus, Raj Kapoor, through the use of his name,
communicates directly with the audience. There is thus
in the film a triple bond of pleasure. In this book we
will be often dealing separately with this trimurti or
triumvirate: character-actor-director. I have used three
different ways of identifying them: Raj, Raj Kapoor,
Kapoor respectively.

Finally, there is another factor contributing to
the intimacy between the audience and all the three
members of the triumvirate. There is an advantage in
the popular usage of the name which is the basis of the
happy accident. The popular usage of the word 'Raj'
endows the hero with the intimate relationship with
the audience that Kapoor is seeking. 'Raj', 'Raja beta'

are the fond appellations (pet names) that mothers in our country, particularly in the North (and the East too) use to address the child. There are quite a few such 'kingly' appellations in fact, running into variations like Rana, Samrat, Badshah, Rajkumar, etc. (There are the female parallels too: Rani, Rajkumari or Rajdulari), 'Mera beta raja banega' (My son will be a king) or 'Meri beti raj karegi' (My daughter will reign in the house of the in-laws) may not always be a literally blatant desire, but has a definite quality of verbal caress or dulaar. There does lurk of course a wish for the acquisition of the material wealth, power and social position that go with kinghood. Sisters follow mothers in lavishing love and indulgence on their brothers, calling them 'Raja-bhaiya'. What is most interesting is that wives, too, often call their husbands 'Raja' in private. This practice might have arisen out of the necessity to find a form of addressing husbands, because of the social taboo forbidding them the use of the proper names of husbands. 'Raja' thus becomes part of the verbal idiom of love-making. Hindi films have always highlighted this practice in their songs.

This custom, obviously a hangover of monarchic rule, is also part of a tradition that seeks to raise the loved one to the level of the sovereign and ultimately to the level of Godhood, for God is the ultimate sovereign. We will see later how the name is connected with the romanticism running through the film. With irony, identification, and intimacy, the naming offers many openings. The choice of the name is thus fortuitous.

Not only the name of the principal character but all the names in the film have been chosen with care. Like Raj Kapoor, actress Leela Chitnis lends her name to the mother's character. So now one could look for a continuation of this system in the case of the father too. But, no, though Prithviraj Kapoor, acting as the father, bears a kingly name suited to his person, his own name has been discarded in favour of another. The character he plays has been given a name belonging to another king—the king of Ayodhya in the Ramayan. Usually the heroes of Indian cinema are likened to Ram, Krishna or Shiv. But in this one film the hero is the son of Ram, with at least two allusions connecting the other Raghunath, i.e., Ram, with the hero's father. The nomenclature is clarified and explained in the course of the film.

The other two characters, Rita and Jugga, have names that have no meaning but have other associations. Rita is a Western/non-traditional name; whereas Jugga (which could be an abbreviation of Jagannath or Jagmohan or whatever) is a rural name.

It is obvious already that all three names—Raj, Rita and Raghunath—have one thing in common— the letter 'R'. These three are the main protagonists of the film. All three of them, we will see later, form a 'triangular relationship' underscored by the deliberate choice of the starting 'R'.

THE TITLE OF THE FILM

The Title Cards

The title cards demand the same care as goes into the naming of characters, and sometimes even more. They are only too often much more than a mere prop for the names of the cast and the unit. Filmmakers make use of that bit of film material, enriching it with visuals and sound either to throw some light on what is to come or to give some kind of a summation of the film. For example, if one misses the title cards of Hitchcock's *North by Northwest,* it is a serious loss, for they have a bearing on the structural and the thematic thrusts of the film.

Title cards sometimes have a musical piece in the manner of an overture to the entire sound track of the film; containing a little of all the important musical pieces from the entire film. The pieces from this overture later become motifs and leitmotifs that identify segments or scenes or moments, and increase their significance by the repeated use of these pieces of music over them and connecting them. Ray's use of title music in *Pather Panchali* is a case in point.[5]

In *Awāra* the title cards roll on one continuous image of a child, a little boy sitting under a gas lamppost, the camera set at a little height and in extreme long shot (ELS). A little later, a street dog approaches the child looking for food. The boy shares with the dog his own roti. The camera does not move, the shot does not change. The image is not too prominent or urgent on the screen. The unchanging image does not attract too much of attention, but creates an ambiance for the film. Incidentally, this particular boy appears nowhere again. He can be the hero, at an even younger age than what is shown in the film or he can be just any boy. In other words, if the film does reach towards a universality, then the title cards visuals contribute towards it, in avoiding the image of any particular person. To sum up, both the title of the film and its title cards signify an effort towards a generality rather than a particularity.

THE FATHER, AND THE
OTHER GENERATIONS

There are several reasons why one could begin with
the character of the father, the justice Raghunath; the
simplest one being that a person's identity comes from
his father and his parentage. It is a patriarchal mode
and we are within it at this moment; the film deals
with patriarchy and we begin with the patriarch. With
the same logic, we could look for some information
about Raghunath's father and it is to the credit of the
film that we find that too. Yes, the film does go back
that far. Both the information that we get, and the way
it is presented to us, are quite revealing, Raghunath's
father was a big landlord, a Talukedar, somewhere in
Uttar Pradesh (UP), *but he liked to spend most of his
time in Bombay*. The italicized part of the information
is however unconnected with the narrative, for
Raghunath did not study or live in Bombay. In other
words, it seems a surplus piece of information. When
we see him he has been practising law in Lucknow. But

this 'extra' bit of information, coming from the pen
of Abbas, has other implications. For it immediately
conjures up a time, identified with the beginning of the
rural-urban divide, when money from all over the land
was beginning to pour into the four or five metropolis
of this vast country. This apparently stray message that
the grandfather was a rich landlord in a village in UP
and spent much of his time in Bombay also implies
that he spent his money in Bombay. In other words,
money generated in the village was being carried
away to Bombay where it was being accumulated
and circulated and spent. This information becomes
relevant when we see Raj's migration to the city and
his confrontation with this money there.

The film shows a marked concern with establishing
and studying the different generations in terms
of parallels or of conflict with each other. Radhu
Karmakar, the cinematographer of *Awāra,* recalls in
an interview that when Kapoor had approached Abbas
to write the script for him, Abbas had laid down a
condition insisting that Prithviraj Kapoor must himself
act the role of the father[1]. Four generations of Kapoors
make their appearance in the film. The judge, presiding
over the courtroom scene is the real life father of
Prithviraj, Lala Bashesar Nath, i.e., grandfather of Raj
Kapoor himself. The little boy in the title card image
is Randhir Kapoor, son of Raj Kapoor. And of course
there is the fifth Kapoor in the film; Shashi Kapoor,
acting as the child Raj.

There is a hint that Justice Raghunath had once represented or aspired to represent the young India of his time, when waves of social change were rolling over India and he had let himself ride over the waves. Nothing is elaborated to this effect, but like that earlier statement about his father, a couple of sentences provide this glimpse into his past and his character. These words come from him, as he reminisces about the past and defends his present actions. He says, 'I too was considered a revolutionary/rebel (*bagi*) of my time. Going against the wishes of my family, I had married a widow. My father was up against this relationship, but on no account would I leave Leela. For Leela was very good, and I *loved her*' Besides furnishing us with a vital piece of information about his past, these sentences establish the similarities the father shared with the son in the youth. Thus, if the story is going to be about the clash of two generations, the clash will not be a simple one of good vs. bad or old vs. new, as so many films make all conflicts to be. Generations do share things in common, the youth at all times everywhere tend to act in the same manner, turning rebellious against the previous generation. One generation of youth grows in experience and moves away from the ideals and dreams of their time; and in moving away becomes an enemy to the next generation of youth. In this film of broken dreams and fallen ideals, the past story becomes relevant to the telling of the present one. By providing opposition, the old also establishes the new.

We do not know whether Raghunath had married a widow in order to 'follow a fashion' of his time, or whether it was the true mark of a progressive mind, a genuine passion and a protest against social ills. We do not know how conscious he was of the changes in thought brought in by both Westerners and Indians, largely under the impact of Western ideology and philosophy, so that widow-marriage could become a logical manifestation of a newly awakened sensibility. But at least he was capable of 'love'. A father's love is not a topic popular cinema would normally deal with. In this film not only does the father character talk of his (past) love for his wife, a love that had defied society, but there is also the visualization or representation of his love and sexuality.

An indication of the importance of Raghunath's character and the generation factor (but not a conclusive proof) lies in the fact that Raghunath is the first among the principal protagonists of the film to appear in the film. Again, if one discounts the last frame bearing Raj, on which appears the 'The End' sign, his image is the last with which the film closes. Towards the close of the film, Raj, speaking to Rita, does not speak of love or promises of a future union but a promise to be like his father: 'Last night I saw a father, I liked him very much. I want to be like my father.' It is significant that the souvenir that Rita must carry during her separation from Raj is a necklace belonging to Raj's mother that Raj has given her as a memento to remember—not him alone but the other generation as well.

The formidable figure of Prithviraj Kapoor lends itself well to the creation of the personality of the patriarch: the handsome, strong-willed, Westernized man, 'with a towering personality' and a rich baritone voice. Every frame containing Raghunath is composed to his advantage—till at the end, when suddenly he looks shrunken and small. Many cinematic and stylistic devices have been used in the sequences with him, to make this figure appear grand, larger-than-life, domineering over all those around him. While many of these devices are what can be called 'the cinematic highs', some of them are narrative modes traditionally used to produce high drama. We will follow the film chronologically for a while, analysing the narrative and the cinematic aspects of the sequences as we go on.

The film opens with the *courtroom sequence,* which is shot in high contrast light and shadow, with extreme camera positions and angles alternating between adjacent shots, and sharply focused figures with shadows etching the characters, particularly those of Raghunath and Rita, heightening the drama. When Rita asks him for blessings the high camera over Raghunath's shoulder 'looks down' on her. In the next shot a low camera from behind her 'looks up' to him. All these are conventional ways of establishing hierarchized relationships. Grand crane-down and crane-up shots begin and close the courtroom sequence. Courtroom drama, such a cliche today, was a relatively new theme in 1951. The film begins with the courtroom and all the implications carried by it; the film's very first shot is a low angle shot of the Bombay High Court. It is a borrowing from the Hollywood cinema and the motifs are quite common. The associated ideas/themes could be: individual man vs. society; man vs. the law; justice is blind but the heart is not; 'the heart has its reasons for which reason has no reason', etc. If one forgets these themes as popular cinema elements, one would find it ridiculous when Rita, the defence lawyer, urges Raghunath to ask his 'heart' to tell him whether he can recognize his son in Raj. The judge intervenes, 'Rita-devi, the law does not recognize the heart.' Rita's immediate reply is, 'Milord, the heart, too, does not recognize the law.' Popular culture as the insistent, incessant voice of protest is a notion that many present-day theorists have served to develop. At the same time it is also one way to ensure that nothing really changes. The voice-of-protest attacks the establishment, wearing all the garbs of the establishment, only to be ultimately incorporated within it economically, politically and of course socially, 'Love' is the principal vehicle for this protest. The law, manifest in its two arms, the police and the judiciary, is the first and foremost target of this attack. A study of the popular cinema thus brings to light the desires and grievances of an era. Through such a study one can also understand how a particular social status quo is maintained for ever. The courtroom is the arena where the grievances are voiced, where there is an appeal to the establishment, not through law-books but through the heart. That is why they are never 'realistic', but are always 'popular'.

In Indian cinema the courtroom has yet another significance attached to it; in pre-independence cinema, it is the site from which foreign/Western rule exercised its control; in post-independence cinema it comes to represent all the legacies of the British legal system. The attitude towards this legacy remains ambivalent and problematic. Before we go into all its many facets, we should take note of the fact that it is through the character of Raghunath that *everything* connected with these aspects (viz., of Westernization and colonization) has been brought into play. There lies the importance of this character.

Son of a feudal lord, Raghunath is also representative of the elite that has since naturally inherited the wealth and social position of the older class, and has in addition acquired an amount of power in the bureaucratic machinery. He is, in other words, a representative of the class of the national bourgeoisie that wield authority in the Indian state system today. Through him will be voiced that side of the famous debate carried on by the film: whether virtue or vice is inherited or is the product of the environment; with the implied argument that it is one's birth that ultimately determines whether one will belong among the 'have's or the have-nots. If one is rich one is naturally *shareef* or virtuous. The virtuous, in their turn, are always rich, and hence powerful.

The story of the powerful is told in a cinematic style, that in its use of a highly manipulative imagery drawing upon traditional cinematic and narrative devices, represents *and* wields power at the same time.

In the courtroom sequence, Raghunath is established as an attractive and powerful figure. When he presents his arguments, he refuses to reveal his past even while Rita urges him to remember it. As the film delves into Raghunath's past through his voice-over, we see him indulging in two of the favourite pleasures of the rich—boating and hunting. (The use of the gun on the boat of course is also in preparation for the action a little later, when he will use it to shoot at the dacoits carrying Leela off.) Leela is with him on the boat and it is a little after their wedding: they are still 'the honeymooning couple'. They listen to the song of the boatmen from another boat. Raghunath takes aim with his gun. The song follows the bang of the gun. Leela asks him later why they should be singing 'Beware!'. But Raghunath brushes her question aside, 'Let them. How are you concerned?' He does not bother about people and what they say: this aspect of his character is touched on again and again, providing a contrast with Raj, who is a people's man, 'a pal' to everyone, who wants social approval and recognition. When Leela goes in to change and prepare for bed, he asks, 'Should I come in, if you are scared (to be

alone?)' with an obvious pointer to what is to follow
her bedtime preparations. Somebody else gets into the
room and carries her away.

When Leela is returned to the household, the strain
of love and eroticism continues as Raghunath lights
the lamp in a 'symbolic' gesture. What happens here
is of importance to us. Leela brings a dressing gown,
for he has returned from the court. Raghunath, his
back turned towards Leela, drops his coat and turns
round for the gown held by Leela, finds her close to
him and embraces her. The music changes sharply
into something more romantic (a tune from his earlier
film *Barsaat)*. In the next cut (from the mid-shot to
a mid-close-up now), the couple faces the audience in
a frontal two-shot composition with back-lighting, as
Raghunath talks of love. The dressing gown is a prop
that will be used in this film again and again. As a
cinematic motif, the dressing gown, with its long history
in Indian cinema, is connected with Westernization/
modernization/colonization issues. In the memorable
opening sequence of *Andaaz* by Mehboob, Nargis's
riding breeches and hunting-cane and her father's
dressing gown are the first elements that establish those
issues of the film. Later in *Awāra,* there is a similar
sequence where Rita helps Raghunath into his dressing
gown. In the repetition of the scene the director seems
to be driving at: a point.

Raghunath, after the courtroom sequence, is
endowed with all the romantic elements usually

reserved for heroes. He is surrounded with signs
of Westernization and wealth, and the pleasures
that go with them. We will now pick up one object
that will open up a set of discourse and a process
of signification: the clock. The conflict between the
rational and the intuitive has always been a favourite
theme in Hollywood and the clock has often been a
signifier for this. In Indian cinema, the debate gets more
complicated. The clock stands for discipline and order;
as a mark of 'the positive' influence of Westernization.
It can also be 'negative', set *against* the other sets of the
matrix: intuition, love, individual freedom. Here the
clock is brought in early as a part of the ambiance and
is made to 'play⁵ around in various compositions. The
first time it is used, it is an ornament on Raghunath's
mantelpiece, brought in right after the conflicts begin
in his mind. Leela has returned from Jugga's den.
She asks Raghunath, 'Tell me, is it necessary that a
gentleman's son is always a gentleman and a rogue's
son is a rogue?' The question upsets him. In the next
shot Leela is seen pregnant knitting a bootee. 'Let's see
who/what arrives first—the order for you to become
a Magistrate or the new guest.' Raghunath is grim:
'There is no chance of my becoming a magistrate'. He
is framed by the clock. It is made to stand along with
a miniature of the gas-lamp on the mantelpiece. The
use of the gas lamp-post is an instance of Kapoor's
attention to detail. Karmakar says that he did all the
shot-breakdowns himself with utmost care, going

over and over them. He described each shot in minute detail, looked at each item of the set personally, and with *Jis Desh Main Ganga Bahti Hai,* a film directed by Karmakar under the R.K. banner, came to edit all his own films. After this shot Kapoor begins to compose Raghunath with the clock in the background or in the foreground. This continues till just before Leela is turned out, when there is a montage sequence with close-ups of Raghunath's face, the clock, some other ornaments and statuettes.

This play with clocks, which at this point merely contributes to the creation of a certain ambiance and mood, will be justified later when the clock in his Bombay house acquires a significance, as it then gets connected with the narrative, and also becomes the voice of the patriarchal order; it 'scolds' Raghunath and Rita when each is late for dinner (another 'Western' motif). What I have tried to establish so far is how the characterization of Raghunath gathers weightage by being associated with various motifs, devices and references. Being the father of Raj in the story does not necessarily make him a patriarch. This character of heroic proportions is built dramatically, is associated with feudalism/Westernization motifs and is made seductive and romantic, and gradually made cruel and ruthless. Our hero will come into conflict with this character.

Raghunath gets more and more obsessed with the heredity issue. In a *play-within-a-play* courtroom

sequence, Raghunath loses his cool, when the husband
of an errant wife is tried for some crime. A friend, who
later turns out to be Rita's father, rebukes him for his
'blind principles' for which he is losing his composure,
his humanity and is now wronging his own wife.
Raghunath is shown as a man of principles, and a
disciplinarian. But all these qualities will bring him to
hurt many people in his life. The ambivalent attitudes
towards these qualities are the attitudes with which the
character is created along with all its grandeur.

It has been noted earlier that: Raghunath shares
his name with Ram of Ayodhya. Now his sister-in-
law tells him, 'Are you greater than Ram of Ayodhya
that you do not even listen to the voice of the public?'
The second connection is made with the origin of the
name, when he drives out Leela, and the song in the
background chides the legendary Ram and in turn
the film Ram, 'You have sent the devoted and loyal
mother Seeta into exile. Why didn't the sky rent in
two, the earth split in agony?' This song, which began
as the voice of the narrator, is soon seen being sung
by a group of migrant labourers probably from some
parts of UP or Bihar. Both the songs in the Raghunath
section are sung by people from a much deprived but
working section of the community. The first one is
sung; by Muslim boatmen from UP and the second
by migrants forced to migrate to the cities because of
people like Raghunath or his father. Both songs are
directed at Raghunath; one cautions him against the

coming events, and the other criticizes him for his actions. These subtle scripting strategies may not be noticeable at a first viewing. But a re-viewing, keeping all these points in mind, will open up the richness of this text.

The issue of urban migration is a stronger or more visible motif in the next film *Shree 420*. But in *Awāra* already there are several suggestions adding up to form a background of migrations. There is a direct reference to this issue in the film after Leela is driven out and the film comes back to the courtroom for a few seconds, where Rita interrogates Raghunath. Rita says, 'Because of this act of cruelty of yours, your blameless wife had to leave Lucknow and your innocent children were left to be brought up in the slums of Bombay.' This of course is the most amazing sentence in *Awāra*. Firstly, it could have been put very simply as 'And your wife and child left Lucknow and went to live in the slums of Bombay'. But the scriptwriter and director have chosen to split the action of migration from the after effects of the action. There is significance in the use of the plural for the word 'child' (and the verb corresponding with the noun) and for the word 'slum'. Rita continues, 'One day, these children . . .' Important social and political issues are always camouflaged in popular cinema. Hollywood genres worked consistently with issues crucial to the nation, offering scope for later study. The presence of the migrant labourers in this song sequence, though apparently quite casual, gathers in an importance that is given to a narrator in a narrative, a narrator who calls out to the characters within the narrative by a song, with the refrain 'Beware'.

For a look at how Raghunath's cruelty is visualized, we will go back to the scene where Leela has her labour pains and Raghunath makes his entrance. The dramatic lighting of the courtroom sequence is heightened here to the point of exaggeration. Another cinematic narrative 'high' used here is the *pathetic fallacy*, i.e., the use of nature during a moment of drama, where the elements are driven to react to the sorrow or agony of human beings by weeping (rains) or by breaking into a fury (storm). The violently swaying lights falling on the walls create the requisite ambiance for Raghunath's final act of cruelty towards his wife. An extremely low camera (placed two feet above the ground) shows the entrance of the angry patriarch as the massive doors slowly part open followed by a number of highly effective close ups of both the man and the woman. Cutting on the same axis, Raghunath's face grows larger and larger as the close-up becomes bigger through a narrowing of the camera distance as well as through the use of wide-angle lenses till the distorted face fills the frame. Leela's face in close up (but not so large) is shown in another cinematic device, quite a rarity for the cinema of that period. There are two breaks or jumps in the shooting axis, showing Leela's recumbent face in laterally reversed positions. Breaking of the shooting; axis (or jumping the imaginary line) is a violation of the cinematic code not encouraged in the classical popular cinema. But here it has been done and the result is as it was desired. (Radhu Karmakar confirms that all this was done on definite instructions from Kapoor.) Then there is a montage sequence with Raghunath, the clock, the bust of a cherub, and other ornaments or objects art. The sequence climaxes in a brilliant shot (a favourite of Karmakar) where in a low angle Raghunath's back is in mid-shot. Slowly Leela's hands climb up his back and she heaves herself up to be pushed down by him again. The song begins as Leela leaves, and continues as she is seen on the roads. From the previous use of high contrast lighting the film now changes to a low-contrast greyish composition.

Raghunath is seen next at the child Rita's birthday party. In a show of *coincidence,* Raghunath has arrived in Bombay from Lucknow (the same day). Coincidence is yet another narrative device that has always been a favourite of Hollywood melodrama, and appeared in other genres like the Western or the Gangster films.

Three very important things happen here.

1. *The gift motif is introduced.* A little while ago Raj had put a white rose on Rita's hair plucking it off a bush. Since Raj could not afford to buy a gift and was embarrassed, Rita had told him, 'One need not only offer gifts that are bought.' When Raghunath arrives he too has not got a gift, so he too plucks off a similar white rose, not off a bush

but from a vase. He wants to put it on her hair (quite an unusual gesture for an older man towards a child of ten). Rita turns around; Raghunath sees the other flower; his offering is thwarted; he says, 'Someone has already put a flower on your head.' A similar situation with gifts will come up later when once again Raghunath will not be able to offer an intended gift to Rita. Raghunath now meets the person who has raced him in the offer of a white rose.

He questions Raj about his father and embarrasses him. The issue of heredity crops up again. This sequence closes with Rita's father asking his friend why he has been so hard on the unfortunate boy, who is not to be blamed for his misfortunes and why he wants to 'kill the friendship between two innocent children'. In another show of 'symbolism', Raghunath's hand, in a close up, is seen crushing the flower as his hand rests close to the bust of a crying child.

2. *Triangular composition between Raghunath, Rita and Raj.* Actually this is the second time such a composition has been designed between the three characters. I will first describe the first instance and then come back to this one. The first time they are held in a triangular composition is in the first sequence of the film, when the three of them are together for the first time. Let me describe the shots

to explain how the triangularity was achieved in the first place.

The judge asks, 'Who is there to represent the accused?'

(i)   In a reaction shot, there is a pan from Raghunath—across the table, where the lawyers are seated—to Raj.

(ii) A shot of the judge. He asks Raj, 'Have you appointed no one to defend you?' Cut to Raj saying, 'No.'

(iii) Two quick cuts on Raghunath and Raj, the former looking from right to left and the latter from left to right. In a voice-over, Rita's voice is heard, 'I will fight his case.'

(iv) Cut to Rita entering the door on the upper frame.

Now to represent the triangularity through a diagram, I will reverse the shot order (I have omitted shot ii, an image of the judge inserted within that arrangement).

Raghunath and Raj form the base and Rita the apex. In the second instance, now in the childhood sequence, the triangular composition is achieved in the same frame by the placement of the characters and the camera.

What the gift sequence had hinted at, the composition now illustrates: there is a relationship between these three, a relationship of tension. In the beginning of the film the three are brought together in

a visual triangle. Thereafter Rita is shown constantly
in relation to either Raghunath or Raj. Now in the
childhood sequence the three are brought in at once
into one frame. We will discuss later the nature of this
relationship and the tension. But now let us get back to
the question of 'coincidence'.

3. *Coincidence.* Coincidence, introduced as a matter
   of simple convenience, can become a cliche, as it
   quite often turns out to be in Indian popular films.
   But a coincidence, made to serve as vehicle for the
   arguments, reasonings or propositions of the 'story'
   of a film, would be more of a formal narrative
   device with a specific purpose to accomplish. The
   first argument in *Awāra* is whether virtue (or vice)
   is the product of heredity or environment, i.e.,
   whether a man is born a gentleman or a criminal;
   whether one can rise above one's fate or not.
   It is Raghunath who raises and articulates this
   argument again and again. Raj, born under adverse
   circumstances, will provide, through his own life, a
   case study for the argument. The 'story' is thus the
   story of the confrontation of these two characters,
   a confrontation that gathers within its folds several
   other issues. Rita has her own place in the scheme
   of things, as we shall be able to show later. The
   continuing visualization of Rita in relation either
   to father or to son (underscored by the triangular
   compositions) is indicative of her interrelationship

with the arguments and reasonings: The coincidental encounter of the three of them (and the tension that it generates at once) in the birthday party sequence is a dramatic 'presentation' of the central argument of the 'story'.

Jugga, the Surrogate Father

Kapoor leaves the studio and goes out only a few times to shoot on location; but every time he does that it is for something important that he wants to establish or propose. The first shot of the film, as mentioned earlier, is that of the Bombay High Court. The second time he goes out, it is a long trip away from Bombay to one of Shivaji's forts, Pratapgarh. All that effort had been only for one shot, a composite shot that can be broken down and described thus:

(1) Some horsemen are galloping up a hill; they cone towards the camera and exit frame right to left.
(2) A tilt-up from the horsemen to the front gate of the fort, on which Jugga the dacoit is standing, watching out for his men to return with Leela.

In the next shot the film returns to the studio sets, built like the interiors of a fort. Jugga explains his background soon thereafter: 'My father was a dacoit, my grandfather was a dacoit, but I was not one.' If Raghunath belongs to a family of feudal lords then

Jugga belongs to a family of outlaw chieftains. Jugga thus represents a system that opposes or conflicts with the feudal system. Seen another way, if the feudal system is the established way of society and generally considered as 'good' then Jugga represents all the ills of this system.

But Jugga was not a dacoit, only his family had been a family of outlaws. He was branded as one by Raghunath because of the hereditary factor. Thus, seen from Raghunath's point of view Jugga proves that vice begets vice. But the question arises that if he was not a dacoit then why was he taken to the court, leaving Raghunath to air his theory and throw him into jail?

From a feudal to a capitalistic society: the film makes a simple transition through some representational and narrational shifts, through the use of some visual motifs, etc. But the story of the 'evil side of the society' is not so simple. Jugga is burdened to represent all that is evil, and the argument that vice begets vice; he must provide the hero with an opposition or lead him astray, etc. Thus, the character of Jugga and the events related to him are illogical, uneven, full of discontinuities. He is associated with apparently unconnected sentences, isolated motifs (the fort is shown only once, there is only one vice-den sequence), he is made to disappear from the story abruptly and then made to appear suddenly, bearing marks of absurd coincidence.

One interesting example of such an unconnected statement is the one made by Raj at his first meeting with Jugga at the warehouse. He breaks into English while speaking with Jugga and the latter expresses his surprise at that. Raj replies, 'Dada, I'd met a political (prisoner) in the prison; so thought of learning some English from him.' Who are these political prisoners languishing in Indian jails three years after independence, along with thieves and vagabonds?

Kapoor and Abbas seem to be pointing to a divide that did not heal even after the country got its freedom and was manifest in different ways afterwards. The first stage of the divide is implied through the two families of Raghunath and Jugga: the latter's family is the bad or the other side to that of the good which is the established system, i.e., the feudal system, perpetrated by Raghunath's family. After independence Raghunath is the recipient of the benefits and powers—the fruits—of independence. The fruits are not distributed equally among all citizens providing opportunity for all. Jugga, who was not a criminal, is easily made to be one. The 'bad' side of the erstwhile ruling class is not allowed to become 'good'.

The good/bad polarization draws within itself other sets of opposites: foreign or western; native (local) or Indian. If Raghunath represents Westernization then Jugga represents the natives who continue to remain underprivileged and wronged ('I was jailed by your husband, Raghunath, under some false charge'). Kapoor and Abbas take the help of the fort belonging to a 'local native king'—in order to make this point.

(This last is now an established tradition of popular cinema, where we will often find the desi daku and the foreign crook with their definite sets of iconography.)

The first jerk, the first break in the 'logic', comes when Jugga appears, in yet another piece of coincidence, at the time of Raj's birth. The one function of this negative character is to prove Raghunath's theory wrong. So when the child of the feudal lord/upkeeper of the law of the country/the successful man is born 'by the side of the gutter', Jugga appears out of nowhere and plants the seeds of the drama: 'Now Justice Raghunath, we will see whether your son becomes a *shareef* (gentleman) or a *badmaash* (crook).' Through a continuity of history—feudalism or capitalism, a free nation or a nation under bondage—the country is/was being governed by the same set *of* people. The story of *Awāra* points at this status quo through the heredity question.[2]

It is important to note here that the story of *Awāra* is not the usual story of personal vendetta. Jugga will never be seen in a personal or physical confrontation with the other patriarch, but will provide a steady subtext.[3]

The second time Jugga appears he proves to be a benefactor of Raj, for the slum boys who had been tormenting him fly at his appearance. These boys who had shown no fear of the law in the person of a police constable show great fear of the outlaw. Jugga is also established in his new role: no more Jugga the dacoit (Jugga-daku) but Jugga the don (Jugga-dada).

At the same time Jugga is the evil force in the life of Raj for Jugga forces him into a life of crime. Just as the benevolent patriarchy of yore has turned malevolent for Raj, for his father has banished him and denied him his identity, so does the malevolent patriarchy of the underground godfather lend a helping hand—an evil helping hand. Jugga says, 'Who will give a slum boy like you work? What will you eat, how will you survive if you work? You must steal, yes, you must steal, rob, grab and if necessary kill!'

A later sequence draws its meaning from this sequence. Raj tells Rita, 'What are industrialists, millionaires, politicians? Thieves like me.' Good and bad are not neatly polarized areas anymore, nor is the conflict between Raghunath and Jugga a simple case of good vs. bad or hero vs. villain. In the triangular relationship of Raghunath, Raj and Jugga, both the older men are villainous to Raj. In fact if Raj experiences any fatherly affection at all then it is from Jugga that he will receive it. Their meeting after Raj's release from jail is full of humour and charm. Raj picks Jugga's pocket and teases him. As audience we forget the role of Jugga as a villain and share in the camaraderie of the two crooks. In the vice-den sequence Raj demands from Jugga 'a fifty-fifty share' in the gains from their next assignment. Raj has grown up and equalled this surrogate father, who keeps calling him 'my boy' (beta) and believes that the son will maintain his good name and further his 'reputation'.

If the city is the birthplace of capitalism then a city film will have stories where those who break laws are the heroes and the makers of law are also to be shown as villains. Thus, for a while Jugga is installed as a loving father-figure and a lovable crook. The village-daku thus becomes a city's underworld king-pin, without any explanation or any history of *his* migration. Jugga-daku (dacoit) is transformed at one stroke into Jugga-dada (don). He owns a vice-den, a house of pleasure, where an international crowd gambles, a moll dances, where plots are hatched and money is shared or distributed among his gang. Incidentally we do not see him first in this set-up. The first meeting of Jugga and Raj takes place in a warehouse to underpin the significance of the meeting. The vice-den is introduced through a dissolve on a photograph of the child Rita. We are brought back into the smoke-filled room where the moll begins her song and dance. Architecturally this room is similar to the big hall in Raghunath's palatial house: a staircase coming down to the lobby and going up and opening up into a large veranda that connects the upper rooms. This is the other world of Raj; he does not really belong to this world for he spurns the moll, the 'other woman'. The two worlds of Raj—the world of supposed virtue and that of supposed vice—are not in conflict with each other but it is Raj who is in conflict with both. So the script does not bring the two patriarchs in direct confrontation.

Another person who is never shown in relation to Jugga is Rita. Though Jugga is made to die (or killed) under a photograph of the child Rita and at the feet of Raj's mother Leela, as if such a death can relieve him somewhat of his sins; yet he will never meet Rita in 'real life'. The fact that Rita is shown in constant relation with either Raj or Raghunath but any connection between her and Jugga is significantly absent is an important fact.

THE WOMAN: THE WOMEN

Rita is the woman our hero is in love with, the woman over whom father and son come into conflict, and— the heroine of the film. Her characterization has to be seen in terms of the internal demands of the film. Characters are created for a film; they are made to appear, reappear or disappear; words are put into their mouths; they break out into this gesture or that—all according to 'the world' of the film, 'the world' of the film that we watch. It is the reasonings and arguments of the film more than considerations of realism that determine the presence of a character and the mode of his/her representation.

Rita has been shown as a child and as a woman; a third way of representing her has been through a photograph of hers taken in her childhood. Now, it will not do to think that since the film covers a long stretch of time we necessarily see her as a child and as a woman. We will then be ignoring the fact that the two representations have two distinct functions.

Again, we will get only a partial picture if we treat the photograph as merely a testimony to Raj's continuing love for her and his waiting. The photograph has other functions too.

Rita's first appearance in this film has been discussed in the previous chapter, where it was discussed up to a point, stopping at the start of the shot. We will resume from where we had left: Rita makes her entrance in the courtroom in such a way as to form a visual triangle with the two male protagonists. She walks from the top of the frame in long shot, walks towards the camera, and stops a while in mid-shot enabling us to 'look' at her. Then she goes to the left, the camera pans on her and sees her walking past Raghunath; till she goes out of frame while the camera, instead of following her, tracks a little towards Raghunath. There is a perfection of craft in the way director Kapoor maintains the balance in the overall composition, by showing Rita once in relation to the older man before taking her to the younger one. So the arrow goes around the triangle, touching the three points: Raghunath—Raj—Rita—Raghunath—Rita—Raj—Rita. That little tracking forward of the camera towards Raghunath has its visual rhythm. In this sequence particularly there are several examples of such choreography between characters and camera. After her conversation with Raj, Rita will be shown once again in relation to Raghunath; throughout the film she is in relation to one or the other, never on her own or with anyone else (except for a brief moment with Leela), and right in the beginning this is established by the mise-en-scène of this scene. In the next shot Rita is seen outside the fenced-off area where Raj is seated. The camera is at the eye-level to both of them. In the next shot the camera is inside the fence, so that now Rita appears to be caged in, and the characters are put at par; in other words, the accused and the lawyer defending him are not put in a cinematic hierarchy. This is in contrast to the hierarchy that will be in play between Raghunath and Rita a little later.

Rita is shown as a strong woman in this courtroom scene. She is given the same lighting as the older man; her face is etched in shadows. But when she is held in close-up, she is framed by a gothic arch, with some back-lighting; while that of Raghunath has the usual courtroom ambiance behind it. The close-ups of her face appearing as inserts offer the audience the pleasure of looking at and adoring their favourite heroine. There is a deliberate ambivalence in the projection of Rita as a strong-willed, independent-minded female protagonist, and heroine as pleasure object.

In another beautiful bit of cinema, several aspects of the character are unraveled with economy and precision. Rita comes up to Raghunath, standing in the witness box, to ask him for his blessings; for this is her first day as a lawyer. The ward asks her guardian for blessings before beginning her legal battle against him. The already high camera behind

Raghunath cranes up higher, making her smaller still beside the looming figure of the thespian. His head goes out of frame, his body frames the left from top to bottom, her face is composed close to his hand. The hand does not rise in blessing and Rita, though disappointed, pauses a little before the onslaught of her interrogation. The shot cuts to her entire back covering the frame. A woman's anatomy is usually displayed as a pleasure object in popular cinema and many scenes in this film are illustrative of that practice. But here her 'strong back', clothed in the black gown of a lawyer, blots out the image for a few seconds, till she moves away from the camera. She moves away from the camera, turns around again as the camera now tracks in towards her as she moves towards it. Now it is her figure that looms over the camera as she begins her performance. There are several such effective compositions and mise en scène in the film. Cinematographer Karmakar insists, with an honesty rarely seen, that all the visuals had been composed by Kapoor, and Karmakar had merely 'shot' them—of course, extremely efficiently.

The courtroom sequence ends with the flashback and we see Rita next in the schoolroom sequence of the childhood section. In other words, she is first shown in relation to Raj. She has a father, but we do not get to know that till later. We will see her in her home only when the 'inner demand of the film' will lead to a 'party'. But the entire childhood section begins with the motif/theme of School, and Rita comes into this section within that motif. In the very beginning of the childhood section a constable asks an urchin sitting atop a wall why he is not at school. The boy answers cheekily, 'It takes money to go to school and my dad does not have that kind of money.' The question of money is irrevocably connected with that of education in this society.

Raj, the loner hero of the film, is sitting alone in the classroom. One can see that the school is not established the way the slum has been. If in this section there is an effort at a greater realism (evident in the opening slum sequence) as opposed to the dramatic mode of the entire Raghunath section before this, then this is not maintained strictly. Raj is shown alone, and then with Rita, who, as we will soon see, represents that particular world of money and what money can buy. Rita comes in and the first sentence of the sequence is: 'Raj, you are sitting here alone while every student is buying toffees.' The first thing that we get to know about the school activity is that there 'every student buys toffees'. Rita offers the further information that her father gives her a rupee every day for spending. When Raj says that his mother cannot afford such luxuries, Rita asks him to have some from her. To that Raj's answer is, 'My mother has asked me not to ask anyone for anything.' 'If you cannot ask, snatch it away,' she says. But when Raj does so, Rita calls him a 'savage'. Raj is angry and twists her arm, and Rita placates him with a very coy, almost seductive gesture, pleading, 'No, no, please don't.'

At home just before coming to school, Raj had declared to his mother, 'I want to be an awāra.' This potential awāra goes to school (a social institution), finds himself alone (the beginning of a romantic hero), not being able to share in others' activities (because of his economic background). He finds a girlfriend (the link with the world outside), who belongs to the world of the 'haves'. She offers him a 'part' of that world, she suggests a way of tackling that world; but when he does so she calls him a 'savage' (anti-social). Angrily, he tries to tell her that he is not. But he does it with a savage anger. This sequence is, as if, the kernel of the film. From the constructional point of view this is an excellent example of a part approximating the whole of the work. In this non-dramatic scene lies the seed of the entire drama and its conditions.

Rita jumps onto a bench and there begins now a flow of words spoken and visual signs, a flow that runs onto the next sequence and forms a thematic chain, bearing witness to the mastery of the script-writer Abbas, while the director matches the visuals remaining within that thematic chain in a mark of considerable economy. Tomorrow is my *birthday party*. You must come. My father has ordered a huge *cake* for me.' Toffee, money, party, cake— the iconography of the world Raj wants to inhabit becomes 'visible' now. In the next cut the image

is filled with *balloons*. As the balloons part (with
the strings pulled offscreen), it is revealed that
the camera, on a crane, is looking down upon the
children assembled around the birthday *cake:* the
effect is the same as that of having a close-up and
a long-shot coming together (a favourite device of
Kapoor and Karmakar, but not a common practice
at that period). The crane descends, as Rita finishes
cutting the cake, and the girls and boys surrounding
the table thrust forward the *gifts* they have brought
for her. There is no conventional birthday song to
interfere with the thematic flow identified above, and
the rhythm of the film. The next cut is spectacular
again: the entire frame is covered with *gifts*, composed
two-dimensionally, thrusting out of the frame. The
gifts part (with a little crane-up movement), and we
see Rita's face framed against dozens of *dolls:* Rita is
now completely enclosed among the toys. Rita says,
'Come, let us have *ice-creams*.[3] Cut to the children
having ice-creams seated around the tables, while Rita
rushes around in the excitement of the celebrations
around her, in a show of vulgar coquettishness. She
stops as she sees the child Raj, his cherubic innocent
face (played by brother Shashi Kapoor) in strong
contrast to her child-woman face. She asks, 'Why,
Raj, if you have not brought me a *gift*, you could at
least give me a flower. One need not only offer gifts
that are bought.' Raj plucks a *white rose off the bush*
and puts it on her hair. A Eurasian/foreign girl calls

out to Rita in English, 'Rita, your father is calling
you.' Rita takes Raj along with her.

It will be clearer now why Raghunath is brought
in at this point. After a world of goodies has been
established fully, it is now necessary that the counter-
argument to the *awarapan* of Raj is brought back into
play. After the Raj-Rita relationship has been exploited
fully the third arm of the triangle 'arrives'. Rita's father
is a peripheral figure in the scene. But he is there to
bring up the question of heredity. After this we will
not see him any more. Structural, stylistic, narrative
and thematic unity is crucial in a film made in the
classical mode. Not only do these sequences, described
so far, show an effective whole-part relationship, they
exemplify Kapoor's directorial efficiency in other
respects too. Each sequence is 'hooked' on to the
next, in the manner of a Hollywood film. There is an
overall thematic logic guiding the shot compositions,
juxtaposition of shots, dialogues, selection of locale and
construction of space. The stylistics adopted is 'hooked'
too. Rita's talk about cakes and parties leads us easily
to a disruption of the 'realistic' style adopted earlier, to
a different mode set for the party, which in turn shifts
to the earlier 'high' style of the Raghunath section. The
sequence ends with a close-up of Raghunath's hand
crushing the white rose that he had picked off a vase
to offer her as a gift, as Rita's father asks him why he
has to 'kill the innocent friendship between two little
children'.

The unity within the fragmented style will be discussed later, but for the present it would be worthwhile to observe that in popular cinema there is an overall coherence that gives it its vitality, power and charm. This control over all the elements simultaneously endows the popular cinema with an attraction that overrides all the ambiguities. Popular cinema works with and upon tremendous ambivalences which will be gone into by and by in this book; one of these we can notice here in the creation of the Rita-character itself. This little girl who is to grow up into the woman, who will be loved by the hero, or maybe is the hero's beloved already, is shown to be the representative of a world that the romantic hero is in conflict with. In other words, we can read already the entire story of his future conflict. Though from a superficial narrative study point of view, these sequences are only 'establishing' the past in order to 'explain' the story. The construct can be plotted this way, where 'plot' is not merely the story outline but the plotting of the entire filmic logic/spirit/experience:

(home): mother's loving administration—father's ideology and modus vivendi—son's rebellion against it—the first use of the word awāra—s (the world/society/school)—the lone hero—girl friend—toffee—party—cake—balloons—cake— gifts—dolls—ice-cream—the hero's gift—flower in the bush—father's gift—flower in the vase—the question of parentage and heritage.

In short, a certain ideology and its tension with a consumerist society.

It is clear by now that Rita is not 'just a rich girl' the hero is in love with. To show a rich girl it would have been enough to establish her in a rich home and that would have been all. It would not be correct either to say that putting a rich girl in love with a poor boy is enough indication of the ideology of a film; for whatever is intended must permeate every aspect of filmmaking. After we recognize the 'inner' logic of a film, then and only then can it be subjected to an 'external' evaluation. For example, the strange, quite unacceptable representation of the female figure (the little girl's acting evoking vulgar seduction) has to be understood in terms set by the film—which is yet to be done—before we judge it in terms of female representation, and voyeurism. For this of course we have to go on observing for some time more how Rita's character unfolds.

After the party sequence, Rita disappears *from* the film for a while and the attention is entirely on the hero, his adversities, his attempts to 'earn an honest living' till he succumbs to his 'fate' and to the intervention of Jugga. The next time we see Rita is at a stage when Raj has learnt to 'snatch' away the 'good things of life'. Once again it is not at home, not with friends, not in her own world that we find her, but in relation to Raj and in relation to money and buying. Rita is at a shop, buying something; the image is in a

long shot. The audience may not even realize that it is
Rita. Actually it is Raj and his cronies, out on a prowl,
who have spotted a prey: it can be anyone—but then,
it is Rita. She turns around and comes forward: it is
Nargis in her proverbial white sari. The adult sequence
begins with the hero robbing the heroine. After Raj
has *robbed* Rita, he proceeds to *fool* her. In a famous
sequence, Raj pretends to catch the imaginary thief and
beat him up—a brilliant performance by Raj Kapoor.
From the other side of a wall Rita tries to see what is
going on: we see what she cannot. Raj returns the purse
to Rita who apologizes. 'And I had taken you for a
thief!' Raj replies, 'It is not your fault, with the way my
face is.' Raj Kapoor gives a very good performance for
his audience inside (i.e., Rita) and outside (i.e., us) the
film; the only difference being that Rita cannot see him
and is fooled into believing him in the act. Once again,
according to the 'formulae' of the popular cinema the
humour is sharpened when the events taking place
in the ignorance of a character, while the audience
obviously gets to know/see.[1]

    Running away from the law, Raj enters Rita's house
after having fooled the guard (once again Raj Kapoor
is excellent). The house Rita stays in is important now:
for it is the house where both she and Raghunath live.
Somewhere along this time, her father has died, she
has never had a mother (in the film), and Raghunath
has become her guardian; so she has come to live in
Bombay, a set of facts, casually slipped into the film.

There may lie a simple explanation in the fact that it is a film about a male hero. But the character of Rita is of no little importance in the film, so there must be other 'reasons'. If *Awāra* is a love story and the story is about two young, socially disparate people wanting to unite and the family/elders/society standing in opposition to this unity then Rita's father could very well have provided the opposition. Why did Raghunath have to be put there as her father in the first place? As one looks for an answer to this question, one can see that the director/scriptwriter chose not to adopt the easier, more realistic, more logical means. One 'explanation' for the heroine not having a mother lies in a common convention of the films of that time, that tended to make their 'strong heroines' motherless, e.g., in Mehboob's *Andaaz*, Nitin Bose's *President*, Gyan Mukherji's *Kismet*; or orphans, as in Shantaram's *Kunku*. The fact of having no mother is more than a biographical information; these films never mention or refer to their heroines' mothers. In *President*, the heroine is always framed beneath her father's photograph. She had adopted the patriarchal mould but has to struggle out of it. In *Andaaz*, Nargis has to battle against three males (father/lover/husband).

The representation of the woman as 'the other' of the male, through whom all the male problems and sorrows find release, must be 'free' of the female world, or else the narrative gets complicated. She is created, shaped and explained by the male world and is to be

understood in terms of this world. In turn the study
of the woman reveals the male world and explains it;
for, if Rita is surrounded by certain objects, it does not
mean that she is worldly but that the society has gone
from the feudal to the capitalistic, consumeristic mode.

We are now to witness Raj's first visit to the house
of Rita and Raghunath, though he does not know it
(and we do partially, for we have noticed the plaque
saying that the house belongs to the Hon. Justice
Raghunath, and have noticed too that Raj has not). It
is an important event and in a low shot the door opens
with a flourish of music. Here we have an instance of
Kapoor's criticism of his own cinema. Raj enters with
his hands stretched, taking in everything. He quips,
'Such a big house and it belongs to a judge!' The set
is exaggerated in accord with the already established
rule of 'the indecent display of wealth'. If it had not
been so, if the house had been only 'moderately' lavish,
Raj's criticism would have been directed at the judge
alone. But because of this exaggeration, the comment
now spills over to touch the film itself. Once again
Kapoor gives us a proof of this when Rita comes
down from her room upstairs in a frock. A little later
Raj tells her, 'You a lawyer! I had taken you for a
schoolgirl.' She could have appeared in her white sari;
but there are three departures in the film, when she
is made to wear something other than that, and each
time the departure is significant. Here she becomes
the butt of Raj's derision, shared by the entire film

practice of India, where 'the pursuit of whiteness'[2] is not only a matter of thematic consideration, but itself a mode of selling. The audience too, following the game of consumerism, shares in this derision of their favourite heroine, while savouring what has been given to them. So through the character, the actor Raj Kapoor directs a dig at his own self as director. In this sequence what is to be noticed is the presence of the actor and the director rising over the character. In order to address the audience directly, the popular cinema, in one of its most attractive features, lets the actor displace the character he is playing. The climax within this order comes when for the first time in a series of such usages Raj Kapoor tells Rita after the servant mistakes him for a piano tuner, 'It is not his fault, with the way my face is,' as he tries to explain the misunderstanding away.

The flippantly humorous tone of this sequence, with a Chaplinesque little speech in between, ends with Raj's discovery of Rita's childhood photograph. The music changes with the misty look that comes into Raj's eyes: he has recognized his childhood love. We have already seen this photograph in his house just after his return home. He is putting on his jacket to visit Jugga's den. As he puts his arms in with a flourish (the acting mode shifting from the Chaplinesque to gangster style) he notices the photograph on the wall. His expression and the music combine to convey to us that he has been nurturing an intense love for this girl.

Thus Raj and Rita are united after a period of twelve years or one yug.

There are a few questions that arise here: whether a childhood love can survive a gap of twelve years with as much intensity; whether a childhood love can smoothly run into adult love; whether such a vast social gap, as existing between Raj and Rita, will not be an obvious hindrance to this love. If love is an a priori, i.e., if Raj and Rita are the proverbial eternal lovers, and if that is being portrayed through the theme of separation, waiting and re-union, if this love is such that it triumphs over time, class difference and parental wrath, then yet another question crops up. Why was the adult portrayed with such frivolity, through events like Raj robbing Rita, Raj fooling Rita; Raj mocking Rita, etc.? Also, why is Rita so closely connected with the money motif? Lastly, why is the pleasure element (or voyeurism) so attached to the representation of women?

Again, when love is intense between them, Rita is unthinkingly in love, knowing no hesitation. She says, 'All I know is that you are you, and I am yours.' Later, when she finds out about Raj's criminal history, she says, 'Whether good or bad, you are mine and I am yours.' Raj asks, 'And what about all my sins and blemishes?' Rita answers, 'I will consider them as sindoor to put in the parting of my hair.' But of course as the new woman image of Indian cinema, she does not sit passively with that sindoor on her head and

forehead, but fights a legal battle for him. If society
has abandoned Raj or has pushed him towards sin,
then Rita is the one who has accepted him totally,
unconditionally and is helping him to come away from
the path of sin. If society is male, then this woman is
the feminine 'other', not only of Raj but of the entire
society. Male cinema depends on a woman figure to
restore balance and order into man's world spoilt by
himself or by other men, even as it blames the woman
for much of his misery, giving rise to considerable
ambivalence in the process. The constant use of the
figure of the woman as the metaphor, either for man's
desires or ambitions or for his failures and fears is
a practice taken to an undesirable excess. Though
this abuse, both of the medium of cinema and of the
image of women, is unacceptable to us, I have decided
to study this aspect in this film and not theorize about
this abuse—which will be the work for another book.
For more on love, the use of love in cinema and the
role of the women figures in this business of loving,
we will go on to the next chapter; but before that
we will discuss briefly the other women characters
of *Awāra*.

The second most important character in the film is
that of the mother, portrayed as the conventional ideal
mother, 'good', guiltless, submissive and sacrificing,
quite in keeping with the recent discussion about the
portrayal of mothers in Indian cinema. At the same
time, Kapoor does not spare his barbed humour.

Leela faints on seeing Jugga, and Jugga sneers at her, 'Coward woman!'

She is the upholder of the patriarchal order. It is a litany with her that Raj must study to become 'first an advocate, then a judge and then a magistrate—just like his father'. At the end of the film it is this wish of hers that is fulfilled. The continuation of the male order is blessed by the mother's wishes. Talking about melodrama that portrays mothers, Ann Kaplan, the feminist critic, writes, 'In the films, the mother often gives birth out of wedlock *(in* Awāra *the birth is not out of wedlock, but is suspected to be one)*, sacrifices herself for the welfare of her male child, seeking to elevate him in society or to return him to his noble lineage (through his father), while debasing and absenting herself.'[3]

What is of importance and interest here is that Kapoor seems to adhere to the tradition but at the same time angrily 'punishes' this mode of representing a mother. The mother is loved, as all mothers are, yet very subtly she is shown as an imperfect being lacking the perfection he is seeking. When Raj takes a beating from Jugga, Leela crouches in a corner; her only action is to raise her hands in plea. She is framed between Jugga's parted legs. Jugga pins him down under the photograph of the child Rita. And here Jugga's knife falls from his hand and finally Raj is able to kill his adversary.

Leela has a violent end. But the violence to her is enhanced as her entire face is covered with a bandage, so that she is denied a final confrontation with her husband and also denied the 'opportunity to be begged for forgiveness by him'. Till the end she keeps calling him 'Lord' (though in the beginning of the film she had not been doing so). As an ideal mother she is not even capable of helping her son to change; she tells Rita, 'My son is not bad but he has just gone astray. Only you can bring him to the right path; he needs your help.'

Another female character in *Awāra* is Raghunath's widowed sister-in-law who, on the lines of a popular vilification of woman seems to be proving that 'a woman is a woman's worst enemy'. Her main function in the film is to establish the parallel of Ram in Raghunath and thus her role is important. She also serves to cater to popular sentiments through sentences like 'woman's honour is like a clay pot; once broken it cannot be mended'. She is a popular stereotype.

The use of the moll in Jugga's vice-den sequence is another stereotypical usage, representing the entire underworld of a metropolis—a world with an international flavour: Latin American music, castanets *et al,* American jacket, Humphrey Bogart cap, and Coca-Cola; Chinese, Philippine sailors, etc. Raj does not really belong to this world. So she asks, 'Why do you spurn me? . . . Come, for the season is just right.'

The figure of woman stands as the signifier for the male other. There is now a lot of discussion around the abuse of the figure of woman in this process of accumulation of various signifiers. Instead of showing any shock or dismay at this, I would like to see first how this 'other' takes shape and reveals the male subject. I would like to see where these signifiers tend to go and how they disperse into other significations. I feel convinced that the male filmmakers we are concerned with were not exactly unaware of this business of abuse. If there is the moll in this film, in this book I do not want to despair over the system that creates dancing girls or prostitutes; nor am I looking at it from the point of view of realism: 'such girls do exist, so the director is showing them'. My intention will be to investigate how the figure of the moll as a signifier, together with all the others, like the mother, the lover, etc., also construct masculinity in Indian cinema and give it voice; and then listen to what that voice has to tell us.

LOVE AND ROMANCE

In the classical or popular or male cinema (any of these denominations could apply to *Awāra),* there is an almost obsessive concern with love. David Bordwell cites the American example:

'Classical film has at least two lines of action, both causally linking the same group of characters. Almost invariably one of these lines of action involves heterosexual romantic love. This is of course not a startling news. Of the one hundred films in the US, ninety-five involve romance in at least one line of action, while eighty-five made that the principal line of action. Screenplay manuals stress love as the theme with the greatest human appeal. Character traits are often assigned along gender lines, giving male and female characters those qualities deemed "appropriate" to their roles in romance. To win the love of a man or a woman becomes the goal of many characters in classical films. In this emphasis upon

heterosexual love, Hollywood continues traditions
stemming from the chivalric romance, the bourgeois
novel, and the American melodrama.'[1]

For Indian popular cinema we could raise the figure
to one hundred per cent—all films have at least one
line of action that involves love. Love has come to be a
constant, an immovable juggernaut almost. Naturally,
the question to be asked is: why is there so much of
love in our cinema? A theme with the greatest human
appeal is a good reason, but not sufficient to explain
the entire phenomenon.

If we trace the history of the depiction of love in
our country we come to face a vast and varied material:
the stories of the Puranas; the two epics, the Ramayan
and the Mahabharat; the Sanskrit drama; the folk
or regional tales and ballads: the Arabic and Persian
ballads and poetry; literature, songs, living modes and
the doctrines of the various Vaishnav schools; Sufi,
and other religious cults; miniature paintings and
temple sculptures; temple and court music and dance
forms; the list can go on. At the turn of the century
there were major romantic movements in nearly
all the vernaculars, naturally influencing cinema.
The most visible and remarkable influence on early
cinema seems to have been the Vaishnav literature,
the late nineteenth and early twentieth century Bengali
novels, and mythological stories; but the most durable
influence came from Urdu poetry and the two major

romantic movements of the Hindi belt—'Rahasyabad' and 'Chhayabad'. Many major and minor poets of the time had joined the industry and have left the mark of those traditions on the dialogues and songs. The lyricist of the film we are concerned with here, the Marxist poet Shailendra, is one such example. The literary influence is quite obvious, though a more systematic research could open up other dimensions.

In the first three decades of the popular Indian sound cinema, while the story was determined by the demands of the genre, the songs and sometimes the dialogues drew on literary traditions; and could thus create an area of serious contemplation around the experience of love, rising above and beyond the a priori conditions laid down for the story and the unnatural demands made by the producer who would only too often ask for eight songs and three dance numbers! The staying power of most of these early films and the nostalgic feelings they conjure up derive from their innate romanticism.

But the traditional or modern literary influence on early Indian cinema has been generally ignored and there are many who believe that the depiction of love in our cinema comes directly from Hollywood. Though partially true, this view ignores the many traditions of narration in the country that deal with 'love'. Those who make the allegation are those who see the foreign touch in everything unacceptable. I have met sociologists who are convinced that no form of individualism is possible in Indian society; hence all depiction of love and romance is bound to be imported and can serve only to provide the audience with a taste of escapism. The talk of escapism itself becomes a juggernaut, from which it is difficult to escape. The psychological reason offered by many psychologists is 'repression', because a free exercise of love and sex is not sanctioned in Indian society. So the viewing of these activities becomes necessary or compulsive. These sociological and psychological readings are valid within their own terms, but do not provide a complete rationale for the phenomenon.

Besides, both these lines of reasoning take love for an absolute and deny it the status that the reading of love as an allegory can give us. While the experience of love or its depiction in art and literature is not something new to our society, there have been developments and changes in society's mental perception and contemplation of the theme, and in its expression and manifestation in the arts. In the cinema too the representation of love has undergone many changes. The soulful-eyed intense hero, the crazy effervescent jumping jack heroes, the angry young heroes—the typology changes. While there are films that claim that love is 'out of fashion' and violence is 'in', there are others that claim that love is back; in their affirmation and negation alike they all reinforce the importance of the theme. But why the constant change in the representation of this 'constant' if it has nothing to do with changing times? Working backwards, we can see how love has been a theme through which society talks about itself and the changes it goes through. In one of the most celebrated films of the time when consumerism had just appeared on the scene *(Devdas,* 1936/39), the modern hero, driven by a strange destructibility, fails to consummate any relationship and eventually falls prey to consumption, the illness that was a metaphor. How does such a man become an archetypal hero for the country as a whole for a given period? Just because his is an interesting love story? Consummation and consumption become intermeshed in its 'story' and the film reaches a contemporary truth that is denied proper recognition, and 'Devdas' becomes a word for jilted (was he jilted?) lovers for generations afterwards.

Love has not possessed the same meaning in all ages. The absence of an umbrella term in Sanskrit, in the way 'love' is in English, must mean something. The ancient texts touch on a wide range of love experiences from polygamous to monogamous, covering a period before the definition of love settles down to the monogamous heterosexual. While 'abnormal' love appears in temple sculpture, old paintings and several old texts, it comes to be totally discarded at a point in time. At a still later stage, the allegory of love in Vaishnav literature relates human love to the sacred and gives it transcendental status, bringing together in the process psychoanalysis and aesthetics—conjuring up an aesthetic of love played out, performed, sung and incorporated into a mode of living. What the popular cinema has inherited is a vulgarized version of this aesthetic of love now turned into a rhetoric in its own right. The mechanics of vulgarization that lies behind the rhetoric has to be freshly comprehended and re-read in the manner in which the old texts are read now, not colouring them from over-enthusiasm, and remaining aware all the time of the needs that compel us to return to these texts and myths and allegories. That should be the methodology for a new reading of our old films. Sublimation and vulgarization are the two extreme processes that take place in a medium of group mass culture—in Leelas, Jatras, the carnivals, and now in popular cinema. While studying kitsch we become aware of 'inspired kitsch' too. For years we have neglected to take a serious look at popular cinema from the assumption that it is only high art (whatever that is for a society) that is worth serious attention. It is only recently that we have woken up to the need to address ourselves to both high art and low art with the same rigour.

So I repeat once more my refrain in this book— the need for understanding. We must understand the banality, perversity or vulgarity of the use of love, and its sublimation as well. We must understand the phenomenon in emotional, intellectual, psychological and philosophical terms, as well as in terms of sexual politics. We must understand our own love before studying 'love' in films. And while we face the question as we treat those films that evoke the nostalgic feeling that 'they do not make such films anymore' we might be facing a possibility that as audience we are abdicating our duty. We did not understand, we only 'felt' (and I use the word 'feeling' in the derogatory way in which it is often used). We took our love and loved one for granted. Since cinema rises and goes out of people and comes back again to people, we cannot say we are not responsible. If 'good films' are not coming to us, then maybe we are responsible for this fact. Again, love does not mean indulgence. It is with indulgence that we spoil love. Indulging the spectator or being indulged by the spectator always ends a good or productive period of artistic output. Yes, filmmakers can also be indulgent towards their films, and that too is part of the story. The question can now be: Have we not been indulgent towards our cinema? If so, then should we not put it back into shape, scold it back into discipline? With this attitude I would like to investigate 'love' in *Awāra*.

It is its 'openness' that inhibits the use of indigenous parameters in the appraisal or criticism of the representation of love in our cinema. In the story the 'loving' might be clandestine or happening behind closed doors; but in a film it is open. Men are free: free to love, free to desire, free to express desire in words, through songs, gestures, dances and action. More surprisingly (or unpalatably), the women are free too. In fact, it is the representation of women that carries most of the load of this loving, the desire, the pleasure, seduction, approval, disapproval and censoring, both social and legal. The foreignness or alienness of this whole business lies in the fact that the voice of the woman is heard, her presence felt, her self-determined (albeit from the male point of view). The fascination lies there too. The acts of the divinities, and all the earlier practices and stories and myths are considered things of a mythical past, so that whatever happens *now* could be marked foreign, whereas the West functions within an unbroken continuity that allows the myths and the gods to go on living into present time; in other words, the history of allegory continues in the West, and is aborted in India. At another level, maybe the more intense and immediate connection between cinema and society make the 'openness' more dangerous, and therefore 'foreign'.

Behind it all there was yet another ironic interplay— part of that process that drives men periodically to try to arrive: at some new consciousness for themselves by endowing women with consciousness, free-will and a voice; though in social practice they might be still denying all that to the other sex. Stanley Cavell writes,

'Our films may be understood as parables of a phase of the development of consciousness at which the struggle is for the reciprocity or equality of consciousness between a woman and a man, a study of the conditions under which this fight for recognition (as Hegel put it) or demand for acknowledgement (as I have put it) is a struggle for mutual freedom, especially of the views each holds of the other. This gives the firms of *our* genre a Utopian cast. They harbour a *vision* which *they know cannot be fully* domesticated, inhabited in the world we know. *They are romances*'[2]

In *Awāra* the female consciousness at times is at its highest (so do we call it foreign/videshi?); and at times the heroine is devoid of any consciousness whatsoever (so do we call it Indian/deshi?). Raj had loved as a child; had suffered because of the separation; had kept the memory of this childhood love alive throughout the period of separation. He was the one to recognize her when they met again in adulthood. Absolutely nothing is known of her love, her waiting or her aspirations through love. She merely fulfils the conditions of love as the situations arise. But when the situation does arise she 'plunges' right in. And when she is in it, in the situation of love, she has no qualms, no hesitation, no nightmares. All this can be seen as a passivity. But more than a flaw, it is part of a terribly sexist slant as it grows from within the patriarchal mode in which the text is located. In fact we are still reading the text from the male viewpoint. Approached from that viewpoint, the character of Rita is the product of a male filmmaker's effort to endow the woman with a consciousness that only articulates man's perception of ideals and 'lacks', and not hers if she were truly free.

This quality in the character of Rita is dealt at length in the first love scene of the film. The time is a little before sunset. In ELS, Rita and Raj are seen frolicking on the beach, till the shot cuts to a studio set (a standard practice of the Bombay Studio System— to establish a scene by an outdoor location and then to bring the scene inside the studio—a practice that more often than not causes a jarring visual effect, and only occasionally produces some unusual structural or thematic effect as accomplished in this film).

This entire love scene can be further segmented into three sections:

(1) the swimming pool sequence;
(2) the changing of clothes on the sands;
(3) the boat sequence.

The swimming pool sequence begins from the first cut after the outdoor shot in ELS. Nargis is poised on a rock, before she gives a neat dive, in a sequence famous for its view of Nargis in a swimming costume. The pleasure elements are used full blast here. The tiara on her hair and the backlight create the halo and glitter of 'stars' around the female star. But over-emphasis on the pleasure elements have deterred us from looking into the solidity of its thematic preoccupation, without which the pleasure always dies an untimely death.

Both the water sequences—1 and 3—use the analogy of water, with its associations of boating, sinking, plunging, etc., to lead on to suggestions around the Raj–Rita love, with Rita's first plunge into the water serving for an obvious metaphor for her plunge into love. In the first sequence, there is very little dialogue, but the single exchange itself points unmistakably to their relationship. After Rita's first plunge into the water, it becomes a play of pursuit and capture played by the two. At one point Raj, in the water, stretches his hand towards Rita. Rita teases him, 'The water's deep, you'll drown.' Raj retorts, 'If I do, I'll take you along.' It is Rita's superiority in the game that comes out most clearly. A game of passion which through the performance of Nargis and Raj Kapoor becomes a cinema of seduction for the audience. But is it all just a mindless deploy of seduction which can only be analysed either in moralist or populist terms? In other words, if one feels moralistic about the open show of the game of love and sex, then the sequence (or the film) has to be rejected; or else it is to be hailed as a well-made piece of romantic sequence made attractive and believable by the performance of the stars. In personal life, the stars were reported to have been in love with each other at this point of time. This too has been proffered as an explanation for the success of the scene.

Once again I will put forward the question: is seduction mindless? Does an audience really get seduced whenever they see seduction on the screen? (A pornographic film is supposed to do that for some

people, but we are not on that topic right now.) The
answer is 'no', in that case the appetite would sicken
and die (as it often happens with 'blue films'). The
point made then is that though we have seen nothing
of Rita's waiting, remembrance and recognition, we
see her ready (the sequence begins with her poised for
the dive), determined and emerging as the superior
partner in this love play.

We can skip for the moment the second section and
come to the other water section—that with the boat. If
swimming in the water is the act of an individual, the
rowing of a boat is a collective action and has always
been a metaphor for the establishment. Sitting in the
boat the two of them remain silent for a while. Raj
attempts to kiss her and Rita points to the moon, 'He is
looking at us.' The absent presence of society at some
distance enters the scene on the boat. Raj has not yet
emerged out of his dark mood. He tries to tell her about
himself, 'You don't know anything about me, my past,
etc.' Rita replies, 'Good or bad, whatever it be, I know
that you are you and I am yours.' A little later, Rita tells
him about her birthday party and very coquettishly
offers him the information that she would be twenty-
one, and reach the age of consent. The word 'party'
metonymically brings all the associations of the other
party sequence. The introduction of the word 'party' at
this point is a culminating stroke after a whole series
of seductive, coquettish words and gestures (as well
as sentences with philosophical overtones) directed

at Raj by Nargis, and with that the cacophony of a party seems to burst upon the silliness of the love on the water.

The celebrated song '*Dum bhar jo udhar munh phere* begins not so much as a necessary appendage to love but more as a continuation of the questions of society and its sanction. Something quite interesting happens here. There is an inversion of the respective identities. There has been some inversion already; for Rita has long ceased to be a self-possessed, dignified lawyer, and Raj has ceased to be a graceless tramp. But now in the song, Rita discards totally her lawyer self and wants to hide her act from the society, and enter into an illegitimate act, 'turn away your face, O Moon, while I make love to him, while I talk to him'. Raj, on the other hand, would like his action to be made public, gain legitimacy for it in the process, and make his act an honest act, 'Come and be our witness, O Moon, while our eyes meet, while our words flow.' The act of love may be one of rebellion, and may come up against social disapproval in the first place, for it stands for individual choice and free will and the right to make independent decisions. But Raj (or should I say Kapoor) would like to assert his individualism and at the same time find access to a communal life through the sanction of the community. (We must of course acknowledge the input of lyricist Shailendra who was closely involved with the making of the film in all the stages from the writing of the script to the shooting.)

After the song is over the couple crouch on the
boat facing each other, their reflections visible on the
water. The mingling of the reflections, as the water
surface is disturbed, is. the common popular practice
for a discreet reference to sexual union. Kapoor is not
content with such 'suggestive' methods. So though the
sequence seems to be coming to an end, it does not. Raj
runs on the small dinghy to catch Rita. She raises her
finger at him, 'If you come even one more step forward
the boat will sink.'

'And then?'

'Let the boat sink.'[3]

The final word comes from the woman, on the
eve of her attaining the age of consent. Earlier in the
song it was she who had declared the evening to be
'my first night'. The frivolity of the earlier section is
no longer there, as the full dignity of the situation is
bestowed upon the young woman, who can lower her
eyes, feel the maidenly shyness, and yet say boldly,
'Let it happen.' The sequence comes to an end with
a little piece of celebratory music. The 'dignity' given
to the new woman in the Indian cinema can be seen
as a thin crust on a rotten cake; for, after all, she is
only complying to the wishes of the man, while being
subjected to the viewing pleasure of the audience. It
would have been a different story altogether, if for
some reason—at that time it could very well have been
a matter of personal principle—she had said a firm
'No' and had walked out. Those lowered eyelids are

how woman is ultimately represented as submissive and willing. But a 'Let it be' from the woman herself is rare even in today's cinema. The strong back blocking the camera can be seen as a temporary loan of masculinity to a heroine. A woman with nearly no make-up in the courtroom and her constant struggles and confrontations with both the males are indication of a directorial awareness in a particular direction. In those days of cinema there seems to have been a widespread concern for 'endowing' women with a new consciousness, for *doing something* with the image of woman. What it amounted to in practice, and whether we could salvage some instructions for ourselves from these lost efforts could be matter for another book.

Between these two romantic, happy, tension-free sections there is a bit of a sandy patch. Kapoor once again gives evidence of his structural competence. Not hesitating to disrupt the gaiety, very brutally he introduces a section filled with dark, violent passions; more importantly, a section filled with several references to the various reasonings and arguments of the entire film. Just before a song sequence that *can* seem like the usual popular film masaala, and just after another piece of 'popular romance stuff, a light bubbly section, comes this section, loaded with allusions and references to not: only this film but the history of this genre as a whole.

After she has played her game to perfection, Rita is now aware of the 'rules of the game'. A love play ought to have a culmination in the realization of the love; after such intimacy Raj does not feel the necessity to stretch the distance out again—he looks on as she changes her clothes. But Rita believes in the popular romance stories and the social rules of 'thus far and no further'. She seeks help from society and societal forms: 'Don't you know that gentle-people do not look at girls undressing?' (All the gentle-people in the audience meanwhile have been looking at her partially clad figure.) Kapoor has freely verbalized about the pleasure elements of voyeurism and fetishes in cinema, and has been aware of his own ambivalence as regards the exploitation of the woman's body. And finally for whatever reason when he has succumbed to his own fetishist and voyeuristic urges, he has been the first to lament it. I find this candid admission of his own weaknesses much more interesting and promising than the more defensive, guarded attitudes of other directors.

With Rita's words the film goes back to the hereditary issue and the awāra/junglee/shareef classification. Raj says, 'How would I know? I am not one of them.' Rita, in a very seductive close-up, calls him 'junglee', and repeats the word several times, till Raj slaps her again and again and rants, 'I knew, once separated, childhood sweethearts can never be united again; past days can never return again.' Rita calls him 'junglee' again and now he strangles her—the violence graph rises this second time (the third time he kills the man who calls him 'junglee').

Rita falls at her knees and asks for forgiveness. Why? After all his violence directed at her! We can see from film posters all over the country, the propensity of male cinema to make women fall at their knees and cling to the legs of their fathers, husbands, lovers; to beg for protection, upkeep, love, etc. Kapoor's awareness of this aspect of Indian cinema is visible in a later scene, when Raj falls at Rita's feet and asks for her forgiveness—we can see it as a 'balancing act'. Keeping this in mind, I will proceed to negotiate with this exhibition of extreme sexism here in this film. But for that I will be tracing the history of this genre starting from the films of P.C. Barua, and *Devdas* in particular, and will move on to the next chapter. The topic of love too moves on to the next chapter and gets connected with the question of the 'genre'.

GENRE

One of the most interesting features of the Popular Cinema is that the various components, formal and structural, are found to repeat in films after films. Themes, key situations, types of personages, objects used, snatches of dialogue—are found in permutative combinations in films, often made by the same studio and during the same period. The history of Indian cinema, from whatever records we have with us (and from what we observe even today), shows that as the studios were set up, for some reason—might have been personal preference or the success of the first film—every studio got to be known for a particular kind of film, e.g., Wadia Bros, for adventure films (starring the stunt woman Nadia), the New Theatres for their bhakti films, Sohrab Modi for his Historicals and Extravaganzas, etc. Studio heads looked at their previous films and isolated items with 'repeat value' to be put in their next venture. They sat with their audience to note down sequences and dialogues that excited reactions, so that those could be recycled. Popular cinema created characters who again were 'types', to be played by the same star or actor who would often be attached to one particular 'type' all his or her life. To add to it, each actor/character would in turn be attached to particular gestures, items of clothing, hairstyle, voice modulation and delivery of dialogues, etc. Stars would be paired, their pairing as strong in the minds of the audience as the pairing of marriage is for society. As a matter of fact, the audience likes to see the 'same' film again and again. The audience sees the familiar faces, familiar figures in familiar stories, doing familiar things, saying familiar things. It would be interesting to find out how many films have dealt with the theme of 'separation of brothers in their childhood' and how many actors (e.g., how many times Amitabh Bachchan himself) have been one of such 'separated brothers'.

A cultural consensus seems to be operative in a society explaining the appearance of a cycle of films at one particular time in the history of that society, a cycle that gives rise to other cycles in turn. American and French film scholarship in the fifties noticed and studied this phenomenon and the word 'genre' came to represent a particular cycle of films with recurrent themes, motifs, etc. The most important aspect of these studies was the exposure of the historical and political implications of these films, arising out of the close interrelationship with the society they belong to. The area of these studies has been vast and riddled with problems. Keeping the problems in mind we in India need to improvise a methodology for a genre study of our films; and find out for ourselves how far we can/ should take it. Genre is a term that is being used freely and widely—if not directly, then through the use of terms like the Western, the Thriller, the Melodrama, etc. Humorous usages like the '*idlee*-Western' for certain films made in Kerala are also pointers to this fact. I would like to suggest here that the 'recurrence' phenomenon demands such a study—if a society needs something to be repeated then we take that into account. Here it might also be suggested that it is not the society at all but the crafty producer/director who thrusts such recurrences on the hapless audience, for it knows no better—and when the mass is bored with it all, then they go and invent something else. I do not deny that possibility but would like to suggest as well that there is a dynamic relationship between popular art and the populace which is sometimes violently, sometimes willy-nilly part of the dynamism of history.

There can be yet another reason behind the demand for a study of genre formation in Indian cinema: the importance given by American cinema to the conception of genre and to the various genres and the level of competence that it has developed and which is found lacking in our country. It has also been remarked often that Indian cinema has attempted to give rise to various genres but for reasons not yet isolated these attempts were soon diffused. Before we come to our side of the story, we have something else to think upon. There was a time when a spectator went to see a film and identified or recognized things for herself/himself. Now when s/he goes to see a Western, s/he is going to see something whose importance and meaning is to an extent pre-determined. S/he knows the traditions or the conventions that form a genre, s/he then picks them out one by one. In the process we force upon the filmmaker an intention that might not have been his to start with. In the following paragraphs I am about to commit this 'error'. The chief reason behind that is once again the observation of 'those recurrences.' When a filmmaker is repeating something he is aware of it—the reason behind or the nature of that awareness might remain unknown to us, or might be very different from the ones the study of the genre has attached upon that particular usage; but we will ignore these obstacles here.

In the following paragraphs I will be talking of a few films made by a few filmmakers and will identify the thematic motifs they share with each other; which might mean I am seeing intentions where there might not have been any. I shall also analyse the motifs themselves and attach psychoanalytical, sociopolitical 'meanings' to them. The fact of such insistent recurrence encourages such analyses or such explanation of meaning; besides, this is one way films of the past must be 'read'. There may be more implications behind such an operation but they are beyond the scope of this book. Wherever possible I have also demonstrated that the filmmaker/ scriptwriter were acutely conscious of what they were doing; and what they had in mind was often only too close to the 'meaning' arising out of the analyses.

It also means that I have separated out and identified a genre out of some films. Our genre here is unnamed, though it could be part of the wider classification proposed earlier, viz., the social genre, that emerged after the more precise categories had been isolated, e.g., Mythological, Historicals (Fictionalized History would be a better description), Saint and Bhakti films, Adventure films, etc. Most films with a contemporary background belong to this genre. The fact that Bombay, unlike Hollywood and the American film journalists, has not been interested in the formation of distinct genres, is a reason why we find things in this diffused state. There are other reasons why proper genre formation has not been possible and a thorough investigation into the question still awaits.

That we do not have well articulated, well matured distinct genres, might not be a lack in our cinema. The reasons are embedded in some special characteristics of our cinema as well as in the state of affairs of the country when cinema came here. But one side-effect to this phenomenon has been a marked lack of respect for our mainstream cinema, seriously affecting the medium and its growth. It would seem completely wild to many

Photograph 1

Photograph 2

Photograph 3

The Vagabond

Photograph 4

Law and Punishment

Photograph 5

Vox Populi *and the Popular Hero*

City Lights, a Kid—and a Stray Dog

Photograph 10

The Patriarchs

Photograph 11

Photograph 12

The Court of the Heart

Photograph 13

The Lawyer and the Convict

Photograph 16

Triangular Relationships

Photograph 17

Photograph 18

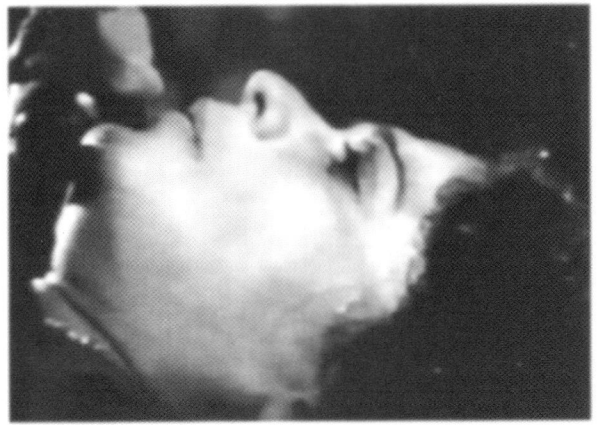

Jumping the Shoot Axis

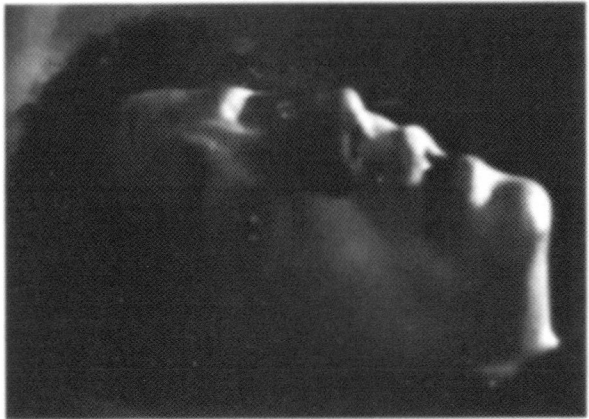

Photograph 19

Photograph 20

Jugga-daku and Jugga-dada

Photograph 21

The 'Other' as Caged-In

Photograph 24

The Professional Woman/The Sweetheart

Photograph 25

Woman, Money and Vice

The Good Mother; The Evil Aunt

Romantic Love

Photograph 31

Bold Love Takes the Plunge

To Love is to Forgive

Photograph 36

Love through the Bars

Photograph 37

The Incest Angle

Photograph 40

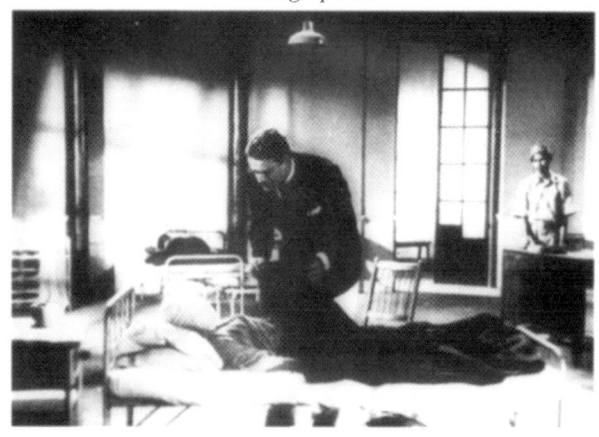

Love Cannot Forgive All

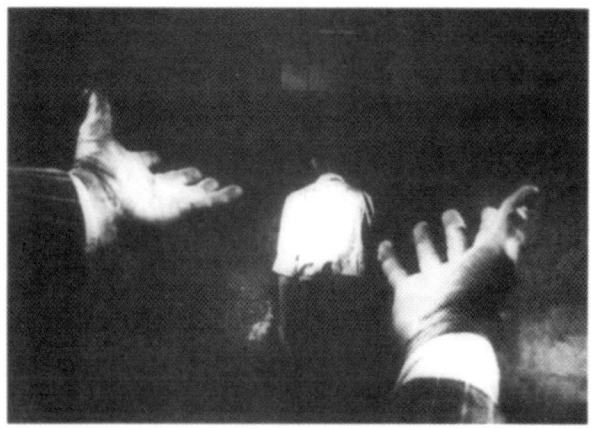

Photograph 41

Childhood and Innocence

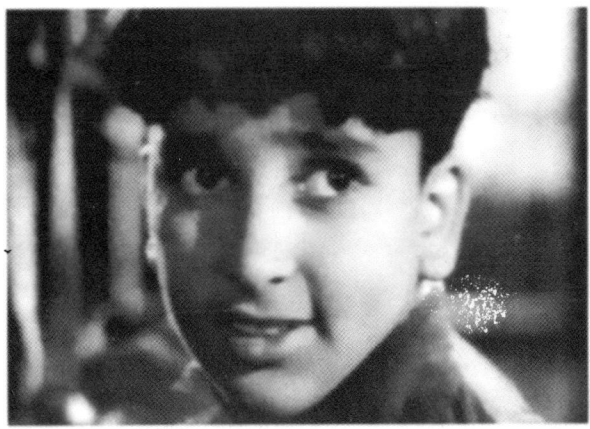

Photograph 43

The City and the Pursuit of Bread

Photograph 45

Dystopia

Photograph 48

The Good Father and the Bad Father

Photograph 49

Photograph 50

Goons and Molls

Photograph 51

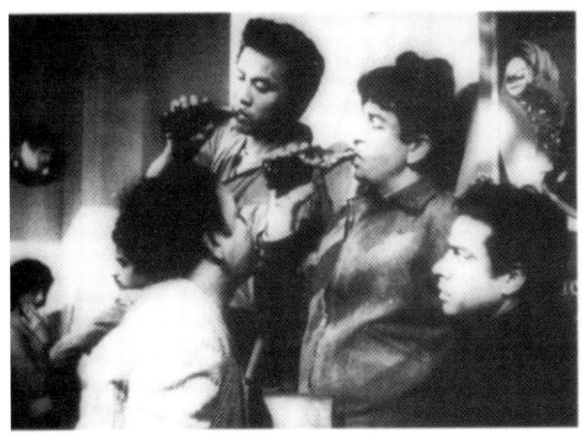

Photograph 52

Gangster Film and Film Noir

Photograph 53

The Pleasure Principle

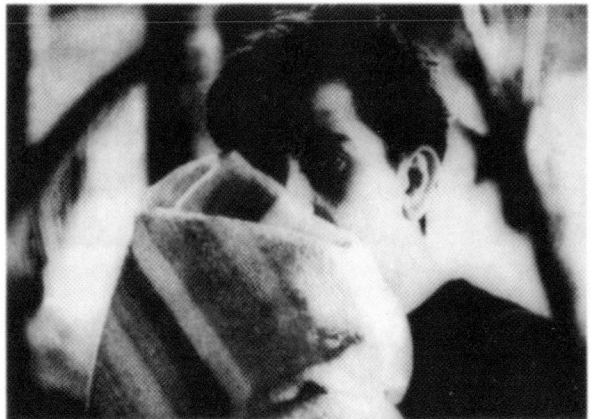

Photograph 54: The 'Look' that Seeks Pleasure

The Pleasure Principle

Photograph 55: The Pleasure Object

Ascendance/Transcendence

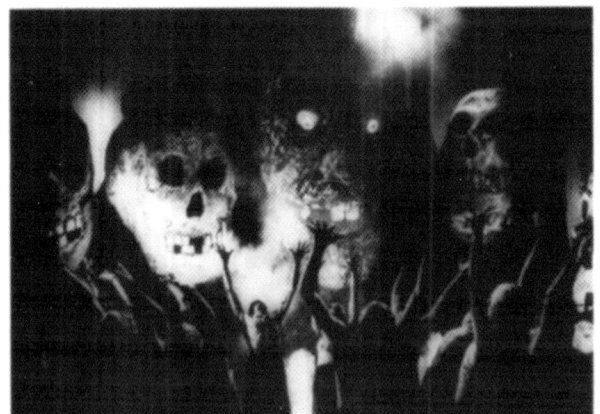

Hell

Heaven

Photograph 60

At Nataraj's Feet

Photograph 61

Collapse of a World, Fall of a Hero

The Marketplace

Gift from Nature/Gift that Only Money Can Buy

Photograph 67

Photograph 68

Colonial Markers

Photograph 69

The World the Vagabond Desires

Photograph 72

Photograph 73

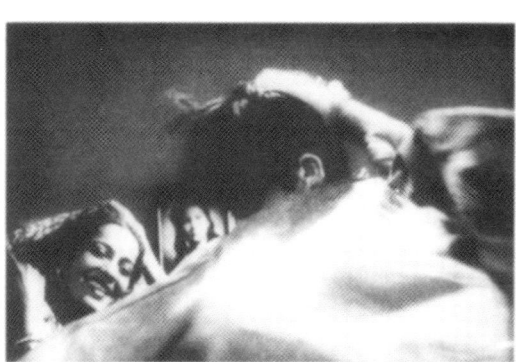

Photograph 74

The Framed Ideal

Photograph 75

Photograph 76

Photograph 77

Photograph 78

Photograph 79

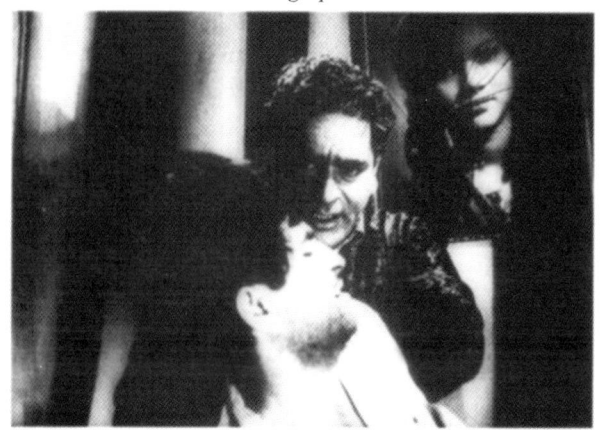

Photograph 80

Photograph 81

Photograph 82

Photograph 83

Should the Moon Bear Witness?

Photograph 84

Migrants and Marginal

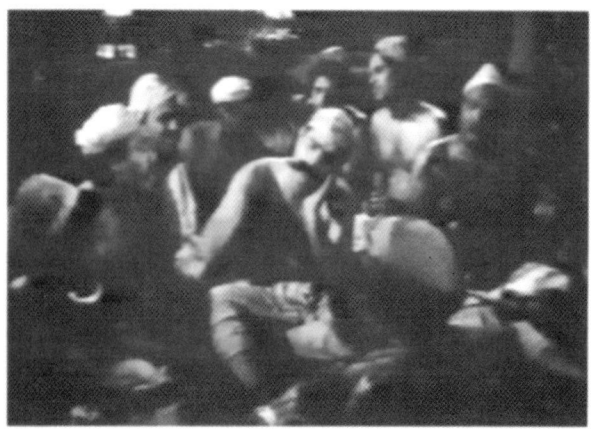

Photograph 85

Singing with the Eye

Photograph 89

The Party

Photograph 90

The Dickensian

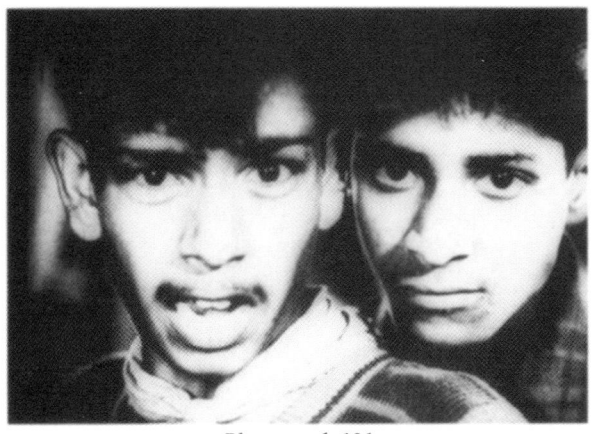

Photograph 102

Symbolism

Photograph 103

Photograph 104

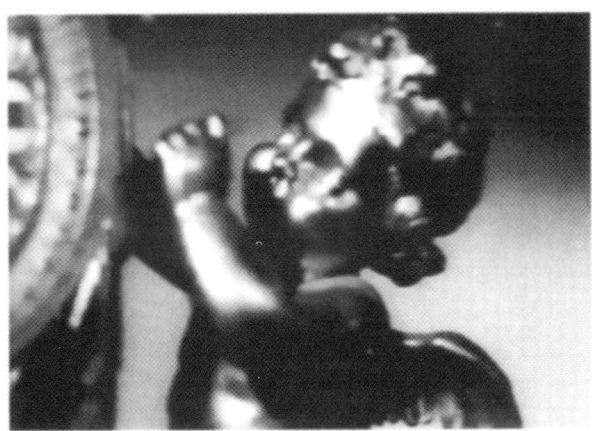

Montage

Photograph 105

Photograph 106

The Kitsch

Photograph 107

Photograph 91

Photograph 92

Photograph 93

Dissolve and Superimposition

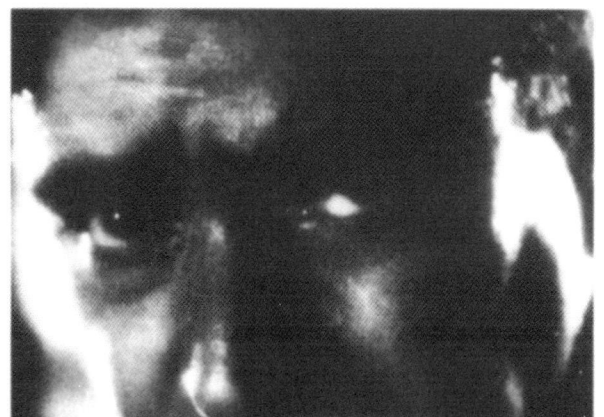

Photograph 94

Expressionism

Photograph 95

The Soviet School

The Chaplinesque

Neo-Realism

The Lover

The Thief

The Music-Maker

The Common Man

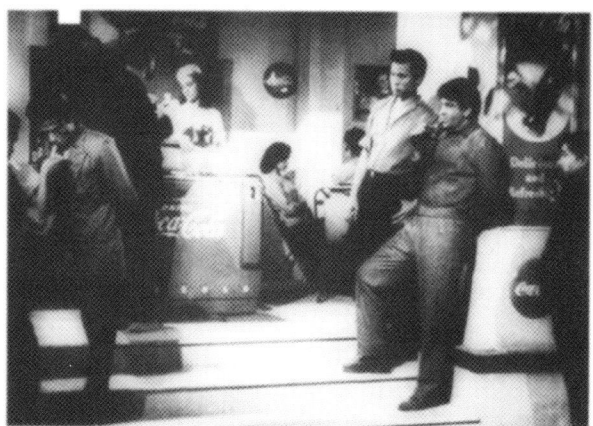

The Gangster

The Tragic Hero

The Tortured Soul

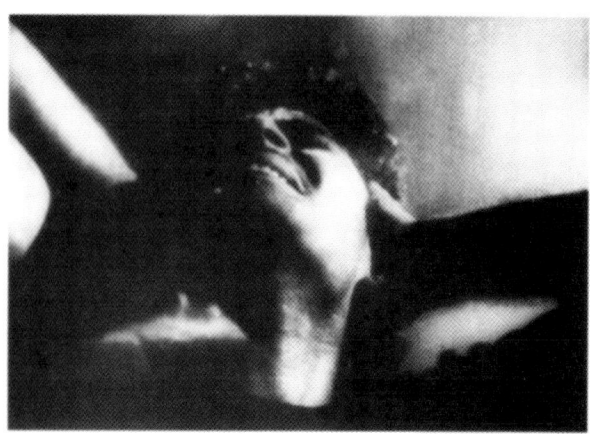

The Artist in Agony

were I to quote the following lines from a book called *Genre* by Stephen Neale, vis-a-vis our cinema:

'The cinema is not simply an industry or a set of individual texts. Above all it is a social institution. As Christian Metz writes in *The Imaginary Signifies* "The cinematic institution is not just the cinema industry (which works to fill cinemas, not to empty them), it is also the mental machinery— another industry—which spectators 'accustomed to the cinema' have internalized historically and which has adapted them to the consumption of films." Not only a set of economic practices or meaningful products, cinema is also a constantly fluctuating series of signifying processes, a machine for the production of meanings and positions, or rather positioning for meaning; a machine for the regulation of the orders of subjectivity. Genres are components in this machine.'[1]

There are those who consider the mass an unthinking, homogeneous body, and would not see the possibility of collective thinking of any kind. We need to revise this position, rooted in the belief that cinema (popular cinema) provides nothing but fantasy and escape. If the social scientist has to write the history of modern India then s/he will have to study Indian cinema to put her/his finger on the desires and frustrations of the Indian collective in the given period. One genre, one component of that machine (the machinery that creates; meaning out of existence), might show one of those faces better. Some films try to simplify problems by becoming simplistic; some others rummage through the ambivalences. Our genre here is one such genre.

The formation of our film industry; the efforts at genre formation and the attendant failures; the interrelationship of our cinema and our history, past and present; all constitute a story beyond the scope of this book. The filmmakers, whose work I am about to discuss, were all producer–directors. And perhaps for this reason we find a stamp of independent thinking in their works though none of them was trying to break out of the studio-system. I will proceed, keeping this in mind.

I propose to get to identify a genre out of some of the most outstanding films of the thirties through to the sixties. My work in this area is not complete and so I will mention only a few films I know well. Till a better name is found, the genre can for the time being be called 'the genre of the self-destructive urban hero'.

The first major film in this genre, which can also be seen as an origin film, is *Devdas,* made by P.C. Barua in the late thirties; the Bengali version was made in 1936, and the Hindi version in 1939. *Devdas* is a major event in the history of Indian cinema and its hero Devdas our first archetype, whose influence has lasted ever since. No other film character has got embedded in the people's mind, making a place for itself in the vocabulary except perhaps, much later, the villain of *Sholay*, Gabbar Singh. Devdas today signifies anyone with unrequited love, anyone who drinks himself silly.

I would now like to present some thematic and structural motifs that emerge out of *Devdas* and proceed to form genre conditions for the other films.

(1) Childhood union/some ideal as given/the village
(2) Conflict with the father
(3) Migration to the city/separation
(4) Fall from the ideal/state of depression of the hero
(5) Liaison with a woman of 'lesser virtue'
(6) End in death/or in severe penance–punishment
(7) Or in a re-union, but the happiness tarnished by items 4,5,6.

There is a sentence in *Devdas* (all my references are to the Hindi version) spoken by the hero; standing in the 'prostitute' Chandramukhi's house looking off-frame, his back to her, he says, 'I am not what I am; I am what I am not. So I must act and wear this mask.' This genre, as it began to be defined in *Devdas,* can be seen as Indian cinema's earliest attempt to define masculinity. Against a background of troubled times, the nation's struggle for independence, this male subject faces a loss of identity, or, in other words, alienation. He asserts an individuality that serves only to destroy himself and the others around him. Films that follow the same thematic, formative or normative guidelines include

Kapoor's *Aag* and *Awāra*, Mehboob's *Andaaz* and *Amar*, Dutt's *Pyaasa* and *Kaagaz Ke Phool*, etc.

Right from its inception Indian cinema has been mapping the history of masculinity or Purushartha and through it a history of individualism. It is no mean coincidence that our first feature centres around the mythical Raja Harishchandra, who gives up his kingdom, sells off his wife and son for Truth'. We get mythological and historical or recreated fictionalized historical (e.g., *Pukaar* by Sohrab Modi), films that speak of kings and Badshahs, who knew themselves and knew their duties, their dharma. As patriarchs, they preserved the laws of the land, dispensed of justice, and punished the lawless. Their wives, nurtured in the same patriarchal establishment, were Sahadharminis, literally 'sharers in the same dharma'.

There were two other genres, viz., the saint films and the bhakti films, that portrayed men who too had their own dharma, which however was not the same as that of the patriarchs. These men defied monarchic rule or subverted it, opposed strongly the Brahminical rulings and followed what they called the path of love and devotion, or the bhakti marg. The popular adage, that came down from the legendary poet Chandidas, was the rhetoric adopted in these films: 'Man is above all; above him nothing'. Films like *Sant Tukaram* by Damle and Fatelal, *Vidyapati* or *Bhagwan Sri Krishna Chaitanya* by Devaki Bose raised questions of casteism and woman's freedom of action and speech, along with the larger question of a freedom that could unify thinking, action and speech. (How successful these films were in their objectives or how they were tainted by populism is another matter for discussion.) Historically, bhakti had adopted the performative mode; these heroes sang and danced, they were scholars and poets, they were strong, determined, self-conscious people ready to sacrifice themselves for their beliefs.

Our genre draws upon the ideology of bhakti as its own ideal; even as it also draws from the early twentieth-century novels and drama, and from the Vaishnav literature (linguistically that would mean both the new urban and old vernacular/'rural' literatures). *Devdas*, as is well known, is an adaptation of a novel of the same title by Saratchandra Chatterjee (1876–1938), a Bengali, who lived in Bihar, and whose romanticism, in turn, drew much sustenance from the bhakti; while being critical of it at the same time.

A very big question to be raised is why, when the nation demanded collective action, such individualism was sought for. One reason that seems to come from the films under study is the sense of displacement and alienation that the sudden socio-economic changes had created, and which was further augmented by the call for 'the national identity'; in other words, there was the exhilaration and joy of forming and belonging to a big nation, there was also a sense of loss of the old, of the regional, of the identity that comes from one's immediate surroundings, from the little piece of land one sleeps on. This history of nationalism was simultaneous with yet another history: that of the rise of capitalism, industrialization, and urban migration. All these create a complexity that leaves its deep mark on cinema. I have seen/read this genre from this angle.

Childhood Union and Some Ideals as Given

The story of *Devdas* is built over the background of a childhood friendship between Parvati and Devdas in some prosperous village of Bengal. Devdas belongs to the family of rich landlord brahmans whereas Parvati is brahman but poor. We know from stray comments that Devdas was a bully and Paro his little slave girl; each devoted to each in one's own fashion. When the film begins Parvati is just returning from the temple and Devdas is singing a love song. Love, set within these religious motifs, together with the Vaishnav singing of K.C. Dey, form an idyll in this village setting. The story of *Devdas* will be Paro's steadfast attachment to her love and her values: metonymically shown by framing her beside temples, etc., thematically shown through her every behaviour, her ability to take decisions and also through metaphysical signs such as her premonition of the impending death of Devdas as she is about to offer worship in the Krishna temple constructed by her. She does not hesitate to visit Devdas at night and propose elopement; she marries according to her parents' choice with determination and makes a success of the marriage, loving the man as old as her father, winning over her stepchildren through love; and all the while she also keeps her love for Devdas intact.

In *Aag* this ideal is connected with the theatre. Nimmi and Kewal go to school; they escape from their respective homes to attend a performance of a travelling theatrical group: the play is about the Vaishnav poet Vilwamangal. Kewal decides to follow theatre as his profession and passion; he plans to stage the same play with Nimmi as the poet's love Chintamani. Childhood friendship, love of the theatre or the arts become synonymous with life's perfection and the transcendental heights for the child-hero which he is never to find in his adult life. So once again the village is that place where the hero is shown as knowing himself, his pleasures and desires. He is in union with his ideal other', the feminine other. The harmony is pre-oedipal, innocent, in the sense of total optimism. In *Awāra*, the hero is brought to the city as an infant. When we see him he is a child with an innocent, almost cherubic face. In another example of the jumping of the axis, the boy turns around to announce to his mother that he would like to be an awāra. There is a double jump here: the shot cuts from a long shot to a tight close-up. The element of ambivalence is thus introduced with a flourish. The scene then shifts to the school and we see how ambivalent and pessimistic is the portrayal of his friendship with the child Rita.

Conflict with the Father

Oedipal conflict causes a rupture in this harmonious existence. In *Aag,* patriarchy exerts itself in the form of the school teacher and the father, who incidentally is himself a lawyer, together with the previous two generations. In *Devdas* the opposition comes over the hero's desire to marry Parvati. In *Andaaz* (a film where the genre components are substantially reshuffled with the female protagonist as the principal figure and the centre of the drama) it is not childhood, but a pre-oedipal early youth (shown through flashback) that had united Nina (Nargis) and Raj (Raj Kapoor), with their fathers sharing the same status of feudal-lordship ensuring parental sanction. *Andaaz,* like *Awāra,* is the story of the 'the Urban'. The film begins and takes place largely in a hill station (Shimla) where these rich come to ride, play tennis or go to the club.

In Dutt's *Pyaasa,* the city hero is fatherless but the oedipal spreads over his two elder brothers, his publisher, in fact the entire city that does not appreciate his poetry. In *Awāra* the hero enters into conflict with his father as well as a surrogate father; the hero is born into a condition of conflict and opposition.

Migration to the City/Separation from Love

The cause of migration, in some of these films, is the conflict with the father and the old order. This is irrevocably connected with a loss of ideal, change of heart and separation from the childhood sweetheart. The physical dislocation thus is always accompanied by other changes. The first thing that Devdas does, in the city, is to place an order for a three piece suit and buy a diamond ring, at the prompting of a family friend, who is to introduce him to other city evils like drinking and prostitution by and by.

Kapoor delves in ambivalences. In *Aag,* the city will also mean theatre and the other arts: as they are tainted by the evils of the city; as his father would say, Theatre is the workshop of the devil,' while Kewal's chant would be, 'I want to take theatre to transcendental heights.' For *Awāra* the oedipal conflict has been pre-natal and the migration to the city has followed his birth. So the city is his origin, so when he meets his sweetheart she is both ideal and non-ideal. Kapoor would literally project the woman as the pure ideal and frame it, while the 'play' of the hero will be with the non-ideal/ideal dichotomy. All city films in this genre will have this attitude towards the city.[2] The filmmaker hero of Dutt's *Kaagaz Ke Phool—KKP—* (played by Guru Dutt himself) is married to and now estranged from his Westernized rich city wife. He finds his heroine through the lens of his camera and casts her (Waheeda Rahman) as Parvati: he is planning a remake of *Devdas.* These films tend to become self-referential through such 'quotations' from other films, plays, etc.

Liaison with the Woman of 'Lesser Virtue'

This genre does not adopt a good/bad polarity. The city-woman does not personify evil the way a moll in a Western does (of course, even there she can represent goodness in a way the city-girl cannot, as she comes to represent maturity, male camaraderie, courage, etc.). The hero enters into ambivalent relationship with the woman. There are glimpses of the 'bad woman' in both *Awāra* and *Aag* (all those faces and figures that are rejected during the audition). The characters of the city-vamp collapse on the figure of the heroine, as in the American genre, 'film-noir[5]. In *Devdas,* as I have mentioned, there is a polarization of village: city = good : bad. The kotha-girl Chandramakhi (who is often described erroneously as a prostitute), to begin with, is considered 'bad' by Devdas (and the film). He tells her, 'I hate you as I have never hated anyone.'

In the film Chandramukhi is shown to be of the same mettle as Parvati. One very obvious (and right) reading will be that like any 'noble prostitute[5] of an industrial novel she sacrifices her life for the hero. But what I am concentrating on is the sure femininity of these women, their way of riding over a situation or stand rock-like in the face of male-created adversities—a far cry from the hysterical heroines of the melodrama. Chandramukhi leaves prostitution as she wills, takes it up as she wills (both for Devdas), and beside her the vacillating, utterly confused hero cuts a sorry figure.

In Dutt's films it is the 'other woman'—one a prostitute and the other an actress—who emerges as capable of love. We see the hero of *KKP* not being able to return the love of his heroine in the same way as in *Devdas*, the film we see him making. This lack also marks the beginning of his decline.

The statement around the city-woman figure in *Aag* is more complex. She is chosen by Kewal as the lead actress for his theatre. Yet after every performance he shows his disapproval, 'You must try harder. Try to reach for the sky.' The decadent artist friend praises her sky-high, but Kewal cuts down the praise, 'Your acting lacks soul; your tears are not tinged with blood.' Never once can Kewal perform *Vilwamangal* or *Shakuntala* in the city. All the songs for which *Aag* gained popularity are torn to shreds by Raj Kapoor. He is distraught to find that their love is no more a love that stems from their love for theatre but is mere 'human love'. Kewal burns his face after this discovery. We see the same bandage as that had covered Leela's face hiding his face now. He 'proves' that this girl's love has never been 'pure' and pushes her towards the 'decadent friend'.

Fall, Self-Destructive Activities and Degression

The protagonists of these films are all victims of their own inability to rise above their circumstances. More than *destiny*, it is their own sense of lack and frustration that causes their steady downfall. There is the romantic element to all this in the idealization of nature, and the village in particular, of the obsession with ideal love. There is also the industrial novel hero with his fears, sexual inadequacies and cynicism Like the romantic hero he is a loner, and again he has friends who are invariably of a different cast, all city chaps, well adjusted to the rat race, etc.: the massage-wallah in *Pyaasa,* the wife's brother, a horse addict, in *KKP* (both played by Johnny Walker), the friend who helps Kewal in the staging of *Vilwamangal,* making brief appearances throughout these film.

It is the way the audience has identified these films and has identified with them is what is of importance to us today. Devdas has become the archetypal 'jilted' hero. His inability to love is seen as unrequited love. I would propose that this could be seen as the state of lovelessness, a mark of spiritual crisis; that is emerging out of a nation in crisis. The tremendous inner violence of these films has to be studied today to understand the violence that has risen to the surface in today's films. The rhetoric of love, identified with the rhetoric of crisis, has given way to a rhetoric of violence the world over. It is also a global phenomenon, an extension of consumerism that: by definition consumes the consumer. The metaphor of consumption (wasting away) gives way to the metaphor of cancer (uncontrollable growth) to the metaphor of AIDS (lack of immunity to fight ills)—this last of course is yet to enter our literature or cinema.

A very strange and not so much discussed film is Mehboob's *Amar*, a film that very clearly talks of the rural-urban question through the portrayal of a village girl (Nimmi) and a city girl (Madhubala). Amar (Dilip Kumar) rides into the village and *falls* off his horse, as the village girl's scarf (dupatta) wraps around his face. The film begins with the 'fall'. He will not love her, and she asks, 'Why won't you? Is it because I stink of animals and dung?' He is overjoyed when his parents find him a beautiful city girl. But then he also wants to possess the other one. In a dark, violent sequence he rapes her (she does not want love to come to her this way, and she knows he is engaged) in a library full of bound, fat tomes and busts of Western philosophers or scholars. 'The rape of the village' is atoned for by the city girl as she gets the two married in a temple (religion once again becomes a vehicle of social protest). *Amar* perhaps is the only Indian film that shows the hero sexually abusing his heroine.

Why did the audience internalize the violence and celebrate the surface romance, gaiety and the visuals? Does not scopophilia or voyeurism involve violence towards the self? The violence of *Devdas* is relentless, but not manifest as in *Awāra*. But in both the films the hero physically hurts the heroine and says, 'Who should I hurt, you or myself?' It will be wrong to read this as the sadomasochism of one man

or a few men, it is in fact symptomatic of a time.
And I would not like to see it in psychoanalytic terms
alone for we must keep it in mind that the violence is
directed towards the representation of woman, not to
a woman. Representation, metaphor and allegory are
all roundabout ways of getting at some truth that is
laden with violence. The terms in which it can be seen
are essentially male terms adopted by the male cinema.
But it will be inadequate to say that it shows man's
violence to woman: the violence incorporates within
itself both the man and the woman. And the sentence
rings true—Who should I hurt, you or myself, since
both are my own creation? It is a statement of crisis,
and I attach importance to it accordingly. It is true that
establishment cinema voices the crisis, subverts it by
pleasure elements and knows no way of extricating
itself out of it. The 'remedy' is in social change and not
in cinema—at least not in this kind of cinema.

Death or Death-Like Penance

I suppose one way out of this crisis is through death,
penance and punishment. All these films deal with
the death motif. Inevitably poignant is the end of
Devdas, as he embarks on a journey across India. The
connotative meaning of a journey, once again drawn
from bhakti has lost all its significance; no more is it
a journey of self-discovery. Using the modern motif
of the train, Devdas touches all the major cities and

towns of India, not establishing any contact with them but hurtling towards a wasteful nothingness. The new Indian identity spreads itself over the length and breadth of the country spending itself out in the process. His old servant, who in his turn had migrated from his little village to the more prosperous village of Devdas, had served the family, had again 'migrated' to the city (Calcutta/Bombay) with Devdas, who in his own words, has been a surrogate father to the hero, now takes part in this meaningless journey. When Devdas reaches his destination he abandons the sleeping man. The camera lingers a little, looking at the train moving away.

Aag and *Awāra* end in the punishment/penance of the hero, both trying to be optimistic at the end. In *Andaaz,* Nina empties out all the bullets on Dilip and is sentenced to life imprisonment. In *KKP* the filmmaker (and actor) has his last encounter with his art: he is hired as an 'extra' to play the role of a beggar and he takes alms from the hands of the heroine in a film within a film situation. After this indirect atonement to her he dies alone in the studio sitting in the director's chair where he once sat.

Reunion

Aag and *Awāra,* as I have said already, end on a note of hope of a final reunion. *Aag,* whose end is more improbable and a patched-up affair, ends with Kewal married to the woman his parents have found for him, and who happens to be his lost childhood sweetheart. In a mid two-shot, the couple face the camera; Kewal says, 'Now I will stage *Vilwamangal*. Will you be my Chintamani?' Nirmala smiles, and nods, 'Yes.' In *Pyaasa*, the death motif is introduced in a very unusual way: the hero Vijay had donated his coat to a beggar who dies accidentally under a train. Vijay is thought to be dead. The publisher publishes his collected poems and the book is a hit. The city celebrates the book, while paying tribute to 'the dead poet'. Vijay appears on the scene only to be attacked by the mob that take him for an imposter. There is a stampede and Gulab is trampled under many feet. After the poet is now dead to the world and Gulab is 'cursed' by it (Why is *she* punished? Is it because she is a prostitute?), Vijay unites with this one woman who loves him and leaves the city. The film ends with a reversal of the urban migration motif: the hero leaves the city, united now with the woman who loves him. *Awāra* ends with a promise of a future re-union of lovers, but under this surface optimism lurk several fears. Popular cinema requires and uses hastily brought about, often obviously patchy endings; we cannot go into its reasons now.

POPULARITY, PLEASURE, POPULAR CINEMA

'*Awāra* is a great romantic classic of the fifties that still stirs the romantic heart and draws a large audience'— this is one of the many such sentences spoken by people in the course of interviews conducted while writing this book. This film has been popular for its love scenes, its songs and the performance of the leading pair, Nargis and Raj Kapoor. The fact that the hero played by the star has been seen as a 'common man' is another reason behind the popularity of this film. The film is part of that legend that constitutes Indian cinema; it belongs to the nostalgia that says, 'they do not make such films anymore'.

What is meant by such comments is that these films had a great seducing power and the audience, the youth of that time, was seduced. Needless to say that the film (or all such films) are now looked down upon precisely for the same reasons. They are nothing but 'fantasy', 'an escape from reality', 'entertainment for a few hours'. Or, 'They had appealed to our youthfulness at *that* time.' Then why this nostalgia? Does 'nostalgia' mean a wistfulness of the hardened heart that feels heavy, the yearning to lose a heart that does not lose itself easily any more? The phenomenon of 'nostalgia' is more complex than that. And why only nostalgia? What about the young people today, who find the film enchanting or absorbing or powerful?

Nostalgia is a homesickness, the need for a home that drives one to look at all the houses one has lived in during one's life. The word 'homesickness' or the business of 'looking back might seem a weakness, a sign of the senility of the mind; but if one thinks about the business of the 'home' then one realizes how supremely important *that* is. A home is not precious simply because one lives there, a home is important for many reasons. If the films of the thirties, forties or the fifties are the ones where the heart had *resided* (or still does), then we have to take both the films and the fact of 'the heart' having taken residence there seriously. This of course will contain the exploration of why 'the heart' had to or did move away.

Pleasures of a past do not make a simple business that can be taken lightly as a 'good' thing or a 'bad' thing. Even if a moralistic attitude guides the viewing of films, it is a little more meaningful than a momentary (three hours long) *fall* or a glorious *flight* (of equal duration). A social scientist, studying the modern history of a country, has to look into its cinema with as much attention as he gives many other things. We cannot go into the status of art or of cinema or into the question what popular cinema is (some answers to these questions have been proposed in this book). Adopting a moralistic attitude on the issue will not do, because what should have been or should be is always less important than what was or is; especially when one has to talk about what is going to be or will be. It also has not helped to talk so much about the 'entertainment' aspect; that people need to escape periodically from the hard realities around them; that for three odd hours they fall into a stupor (in a state marked by the fall of the heartbeat rate, etc.) or they fly into the realm of fantasy, imagination, etc. All this kind of talk is familiar, but we need to probe a little deeper.

Popularity is a pejorative term, held under suspicion by those who find pleasure in what is popular as well as by those who do not. The study of the popular has always met with derision. Film writing today is like a parallel entertainment, trying to outdo films with a different array of pleasure (masaalas). 'Twentieth century critics have taught generations of students to equate popularity with debasement, emotionality with ineffectiveness, religiosity with fakery, domesticity with triviality, and all these implicitly with womanly inferiority.'[1]

Ashish Rajadhyaksha identifies/characterizes the dominant approach to popular cinema. 'The most

common, least interesting one, concerns the habit
of describing aspects of India's commercial cinema
with scornful amusement, marvelling at the infantile
eccentricities of an intellectually underdeveloped
mass audience supplied with entertainment by a film
industry that matches its quaintly simple-minded
naivete.' Attitudes expressed in this context by Western
critics and backed up by the less discerning critics
in India range from exasperated condemnation ('It's
all rubbish') to barely concealed contempt for those
who apparently swallow that rubbish.[2] Now what
is even more dangerous is the use of the term 'mass'
uttered with unconcealed contempt. 'Mass' is seen as
a homogeneous body, in need of *upliftment* on a war
footing'; always an 'other', never including the one
who is mouthing the term.

Filmmakers themselves share this mistrust of popular
cinema. S.S. Vasan, the very successful filmmaker from
Tamil Nadu, who was also a publisher–editor, says,

'What is wrong with Indian Cinema? I myself do not
care for them. As a responsible editor, I tell my readers
that the Gemini Productions are not meant for them.
But as a wide awake producer I take care to see that
each one of my movies become a box-office hit. What
do you call it—schizophrenia? Yes, we all suffer from
it. I have my own formula for moviemaking. I pack
my pictures with something for the heart, something
for the mind and something for the eyes and the ears.
Anything wrong?'[3]

Actually, a lot is right there—if anyone can keep in touch with the hearts, minds, eyes and ears of a lot of people, then he has a knowledge that is to be envied. But there is something wrong there too, and that is the underlying disrespect for a vast number of hearts, minds, etc.

Yet popularity cannot be the only reason for studying anything. As Rajadhyaksha puts it so succinctly while describing another approach to this study:

> The commercial cinema is validated by pointing to the vast box-office takings of its more lucrative products which then allows critics to claim that a cinema which obviously delights so many viewers must be a genuinely popular art form. An unfailing characteristic of the populist position is the constant reference to "pleasure" as the sole and absolute measurable unit of value testifying to the inherent goodness of whatever generates it for "the people". In fact, such a simplistic notion of pleasure implies an identity between the rule of the market forces and true liberal democracy, describing balance sheets in terms of amounts of consumer satisfaction provided in an economy that equates units of pleasure with units of local currency.[4]

There has to be a proper evaluation of the popular, of 'pleasures', for if we love something and then are mistrustful of what we love, then ultimately it is ourselves that we are holding under suspicion. Writing about popular cinema amounts to taking stock of our 'pleasure principles'. The problem is that years of mistrust and lack of understanding, years of undiscriminating viewing, years of unscrupulous filmmaking policies, have created a situation that is not easily described, understood or analysed. There comes a time when we must understand our pleasures and pains. That is to say, there is a time to feel and there is a time to understand that feeling. But there is a tremendous resistance to the very project. I recall an incident when we were watching this film in a study class. A very strong, active lady, watching the film with us, was visibly excited by the love scene in the boat sequence when she whispered to me, 'they cannot make love scenes like this anymore. Even I am getting goose pimples.' Later during the discussions, she attacked the film bitterly for its use of formulae, exploitation of the audience sentiment the representation of the woman, etc., using a barrage of stock phrases.

Mrinal Sen writes in an article,

'Of all the countries in the world we know, India produces the largest number of films in a year. Most of them, ninety per cent or more, are not discussed; they are just seen. They are seen by an enormously large crowd, they create a senseless craze, they spread the most effective kind of contagion and consequently they earn tons of money. But discussions on them? No, never.'[5]

This was written in 1977. Things have changed since then: people are now talking more about popular cinema. Yet we do not really know how we could sit down and discuss what we like so much or are forced to like because of the contagion; and what we at the same time hold in contempt. It will be difficult to isolate the 'we' that love and the 'we' that hate for often the two selves overlap.

Pleasure is not a simple term. More importantly, the pleasure one derives out of watching cinema is not something entirely apart from the other pleasures. We must realize that 'pleasure' is a complex term and how all the various 'pleasures' are interrelated. Just as cinema has been termed entertainment and has been isolated from all other activities, so is this pleasure seen as something quite apart from our desires, aspirations, pursuits, etc. A perfectly intelligent and efficient individual, a craftsman, a scientist, a student, an entrepreneur—all are supposed to turn into perfect idiots and go into a stupor to consume this rubbish. It is true that I have chosen a film that can be said to be a better than usual example of mainstream cinema. There are hundreds of films which would not bear discussion through a whole monograph like this, but can very well be put together in groups and then talked about; there are hundreds that I might not like to sit through.

Even such matters can be discussed effectively. The fact remains that we do not have a vocabulary adequate enough to talk effectively about this medium, about this phenomenon. Some tools for the analysis of these films can be borrowed from the established theories and analytical tools of the Western world, some tools will have to be indigenous; and some new ones will have to be created.

Not only are pleasures many and interrelated; the pleasures rising from different films are different; different popular films produce different pleasures. The pleasure we get out of seeing *Awāra* is not the same as what we get out of *Maine Pyaar Kiya*. So pleasure must be a historical phenomenon. A very important point here is that the film can give different pleasures, with changing awareness. The pleasure or unpleasure I got when I first saw *Awāra,* and what I got while seeing it for my study, are not the same. I have witnessed the pleasures of those attending study sessions and especially after a film has been discussed thoroughly. So pleasure must be something that is dependent on levels of awareness. There is a widely popular belief that pleasure diminishes with discussion or analysis. Those who hold that view have not perhaps listened attentively to a fond cook describe a recipe, go critically over the food served in a restaurant, or a computer person demonstrating the newest models. Criticism, analysis and verbalizations are all meant for increasing pleasure. Through a process of intellectual or emotional growth, some pleasures become redundant, but then some others replace the lost ones. Criticism in practice is meant to increase pleasure, sharpen the mental faculties, and eventually make one more aware of life and its many problems. I would even go to the length of adding that critical faculties make one more loving and less aggressive, for one comes to exercise the same concern for the work under study and one's own tools for the analytic project, till one realizes how close the processes of creativity and understanding are.

The reader may ask at this point: You are talking about a popular film, so why talk about art and criticism? Once again, it is not possible to go fully into the question of art vs. the popular. I could sidetrack the question a little and say that I am talking about a time when in India there did not exist the great divide, at least not in the minds of people. Perhaps cinema was not included among the arts, was not seen as the seventh art. And we are trying to find out ways of talking about the attempts that have been going into the formation of something called Indian cinema, as the newest art form.

I could simply take the position that actually the division between art cinema and popular cinema is an artificial division, which is often played up by people motivated solely by self-interest. Art cinema can be popular; some art films can be trash; some popular films can be inspired. At the same time the critical recognition given to popular art is a modern phenomenon; the place that popular art has occupied in society is also a historical happening and I am doing only what my time requires me to do. Without knowing what a particular work intrinsically is, how can we go into the question of the popular vs. art? This book is a partial and introductory attempt to understand this phenomenon through the study of one film. We could do that better without first getting into a debate of the versus' kind. Knowing that certain pleasures are involved here, we could withhold the debate and begin on the agreement that certain pleasures and problematics are involved in one kind and a different set of pleasures and problematics in the other.[6]

THE HERO'S FEARS AND NIGHTMARES

This chapter will be devoted to one scene popularly known as the dream sequence. I will call it the dream scene, since there are three separate song sequences in it, together with two small sections as a prologue and an epilogue. After a chapter devoted to the contemplation of popularity and pleasure, let us look at a sequence which has often been said to have contributed the most towards the popularity of this film.

This scene was shot right at the end of the shooting and was not planned along with the script, though Abbas had such a dream scene in his story. Karmakar recalls that when he was approached for the film, Kapoor had asked him at the very first interview how he would go about shooting a dream sequence. The full plan for it however emerged only during the shooting, ideas were taken from a couple of Hollywood musicals and it was meant to be a spectacle. About thirty odd sets were designed by the art director M.R. Achrekar.

Madam Simki, one of Udayshankar's lead dancers, choreographed the dances with dancers from Shanti Bardhan's Little Ballet Troupe.

Yet the scene is not just an appendage meant to be a crowd puller, though many people attribute much of the success of the film to this scene. Actually the scene speaks more about the hopes and fears of the director than of the hero whose dream it is.

We shall describe and analyse the scene in some detail. It is introduced by a small section, which is like a prologue, covering two shots, establishing the space where the scene is to take place; with no characters appearing. The first shot is that of a spiral staircase in the shape of a column, rising from the clouds and disappearing into the clouds again. The second shot is that of a winding gradient road, studded with twinkling stars on either side, similarly emerging from and going up into the clouds. Ascendance is the structural and spatial logic of the scene that is to end in a fall. The scene has three separate songs: two sung by Rita and one by Raj. Each song picturization takes place in three different spaces; the transition from one to the other takes place through a climb.

After the prologue, Rita, dressed in sequins, tiara, tinsel stars and shiny powder on her face and bare shoulders, is seen seated at the head of a flight of stairs. The song begins with a reference to the moon in the boat-song—'Without you the moon is aflame. Come to me.' She gets up, climbs down the stairs in slow steps, comes towards the camera, arms outstretched. Never is the pleasure element so exploited in the film as in this scene. There are with her dozens of co-dancers placed at various rungs of those steps, gently swaying to the lilting melody. In other shots they climb other steps or glide down giant slides.

The second song takes place in 'Hell'. Actually, on closer inspection one can identify the three spaces as the Earth–Hell–Heaven triptych. Leaping flames, dancing skeletons, a dinosaur-like creature, a monster that wants to crush the hero in its arms are features of this hell. Raj screams out, 'No! this is not. . . this is not life. I am burning in the pyres of this life; I do not want this hell.' As a romantic hero he would like to belong to a different world; he sings out his desires: 'I want flowers, songs and love. I want the spring.' He manages to escape from the clutches of the flames and the monster and in the last shot of the sequence he is seen climbing up a hill enclosing this space.

As Raj surfaces up from the bottom frame in the next shot/sequence, his head, rising through the clouds is framed by the giant head of a Trimurti Shiv on left of frame. On the right and above him is another flight of steps. Nargis comes down, and leads him up the steps. Her song now is one of union, 'My love has returned home, drowning the thirst of my eyes.' As the rhythm and tempo of the music increases they climb up and up. Nargis leads him up first to another gigantic Nataraj idol. In a striking composition they are framed under the feet of the dancing god. Then the couple dissolve into the idol. Next is the ascendance towards a Devi-figure (identification is not possible as the iconography is not clear). The dance of the other women to the twinkling of thousands of stars all over the set continue as the couple climb transcendental heights, till once again they dissolve into the Devi figure. It is time to stop here and acknowledge the mastery of set designer Achrekar who gave rise to such a vast play of space and perspective.

In the last segment of the scene, Rita is still leading Raj by the hand as they climb the gradient road. She has discarded her dancer's costume and is dressed as an *ashram baalika*, a girl from the forest schools of the ancient days, as she would appear in popular iconic paintings. Suddenly a gigantic Jugga appears on the scene (through superimposition). The journey is interrupted; a knife in Jugga's outstretched hand opens with a loud click; he sways it over their heads menacingly. Raj falls down the path with a cry for help, 'Rita!' Rita turns around, stoops down stretching her arms towards him, but it is of no use—she cannot save him. In the next few shots there is a series of superimpositions over one image: the fixed image of Raj falling down endless depths, and Rita, back in her white sari, extending her arms towards him, while they remain separated by a constant distance. The illusion of passing times and prolonged separation is created effectively by the montage of other images superimposed on this image: images of the idols (Trimurti, Nataraj, Devi) breaking and falling, the giant columns toppling down. The superimposition of this montage continues for a few seconds over the shot and changes to the image of Raj sleeping. The composition here is such as to create the impression of columns breaking inside his head—till Raj wakes up with a cry, 'Mother!' Raj rushes to Leela, falls on his knees, and hides his face on her lap, 'Mother, I will become good. I will not steal anymore. I *do not want anything,* save my mother's blessings and peace of mind.'

Obviously the scene allows for psychoanalytic reading. The open knife in the hand of Jugga is composed in such a manner that one is inclined to think that the director/scriptwriter were consciously using Freudian motifs in this picturization of a dream. Anyway, the scene is clearly about fears and lacks, about the desire for a post-Oedipal harmony, and the Oedipal obstacle that causes extreme pain and eventual regression into a pre-Oedipal stage, more desirable in that state of mind. The dream is about male inadequacy and the collapse of the phallocentric world. The dream, crowded as it is with so many icons, symbols and motifs, is definitely a segment not quite integrated with the rest of the film and thus demands special attention: we will accord it that attention for we have decided not to reject it on the ground that it is pure spectacle or fantasy.

Surely spectacle or fantasy it is. Kapoor wanted to create a spectacle of this phallocentric male world

of fantasy, a world of excesses created to be broken
down. Any ambivalence around the character of Rita
is gone; the actress/star Nargis, exploited fully, creates
complete scopophilia or the pleasures of voyeurism.
The very first gesture of Nargis is the small run
towards the camera, one arm stretched out before
her, lips parted, eyes half-closed, the gold dust on her
body simulating the fire with which the moon in her
song is smouldering. We are now so jaded with such
spectacles and such representation of woman, that we
tend to let the scene go by with a 'simple rejection'
of disgust. In 1951 such a representation would not
be a usual formula ingredient; it is something that
should arouse curiosity and the simple question: why
should a director, who has put in so much of effort to
create a love and its representation on the silver screen,
turn round and smash it so violently? This violence
towards the representation of the woman is seen today
as 'mindless pleasure'. But I would read it as a man's
violence towards himself. The entire film is infused
with a violence arising out of feelings of inadequacy,
of frustrated anger and cynical mockery. The dream
scene, better described as a nightmare, can only end in
the cry for help for peace of mind, for the escape from
all conflicts of the adult male and a regressive refuge
into the lap of the mother, a regression into the state
where desires are denied. He had wanted so much,
albeit things attached to unabashed romanticism; but
they could have been replaced by maturer or more

altruistic desires or anything but this feeling of defeat, 'I do not want anything!' Wanting the mother's love can be seen as a lofty want; but even from such a point of view the film falls short continuously. The mother here has been shown as weak, ineffectual, incapable of aiding or abetting the son, incapable of being an equal.

The mother portrayed as a weak character is yet another common filmic convention in India, a sign of the Indian male psyche. What I perceive here, however, is anger at such representation. This anger is of interest here. Kapoor's practice of incorporating inner critiques into the film while not diverting much from the common mode, i.e., subverting the popular mode while appearing to be within it all the time, is what we have been studying. For example (we have already gone through some of this), when Leela is caught by Jugga's men and brought to him, she swoons into his arms and Jugga jeers, 'Taint-hearted woman!' When Raj grapples with Jugga in his hut, Leela makes no move to help her son and cowers in a corner. Raj finally kills Jugga under the child Rita's photograph instead of at his mother's feet. Leela's end is the most violent of all. She comes under Raghunath's car as she runs towards him calling out to him as 'Lord'. Hers is a punitive end—a punishment for harping on a future for Raj that is most disagreeable to him. She never shares with him his ideals or aspirations or angers. She dies with an awful bandage around her face; thus denied of a last confrontation with her husband (which she is not capable of, anyway—a woman completely under the spell of and in awe of her husband). The bandage in turn denies Raghunath a final chance to recognize his wife and ask for her forgiveness. So, most unusually for an Indian film, *Awāra* is a film that does not end in the resolution of all mishaps in a ritualistic forgiveness. Raghunath's outstretched hands remain empty—in the last scene—Raj does not, cannot forgive him.

If we take a brief look at *Aag* we will find Kewal (Raj Kapoor) telling his mother while leaving home, 'It is not that I am rejecting or refusing your love, it is that I have a different world now and I must follow my path.' Later on when he is a successful theatre director in Bombay, he sends for his parents and meets them on equal terms.

The end of the dream must also be understood in these terms, and not as a run-of-the-mill portrayal of an Indian male running to his mother when in distress. For this is the turning point in the film; after this the film shows a series of defeats and acts of violence. Running to the mother here is an acknowledgement of defeat.

From *Aag* to *Awāra* the gloom has deepened; the need for compromise is more pressing; the world of cinema is the big bad world he cannot cope with.

If *Aag* so clearly had been the story of Kapoor's artistic angst and ethical dilemma, then *Awāra* is the story of succumbing to all that. Kapoor had described *Aag* as '. . . the story of youth consumed by the desire for a brighter and more intense life'—it was his 'first diary'. He articulates in *Aag* what is bright or intense for him. If theatre evokes metaphorically the arts-his cinema-and life then he wants to take cinema 'to the heights'. He prompts his heroine (Nargis) to 'try harder' so that her acting emanates from her soul, that her tears are tinged with blood, etc.; he ultimately rejects her for she has not met with his ideals and burns his face, when he finds himself in love with this woman. In *Aag*, he wanted no split between his art or his ideals and his life. In *Awāra*, he begins with the split (represented by the photograph and the woman), has a lot of humour to begin with towards the world that must be this way. But after the dream scene he loses his humour and turns violent. We must look into the scene closely.

Clearly enough it is about heights and ascendance. But the ascendance to those transcendent heights is interrelated with transcendence in the arts. But then he chooses the kitschy way of representation; and when he does that he does with an excess that becomes a signifier for his discourse and not mere representation. In *Aag*, after every song picturization Kewal would brutally run down the performance and after his decadent artist friend has praised it enough. He never stages *Vilwamangal* or *Shakuntala* with this third Nimmi (Nargis), what he does stage is pure kitsch. In *Awāra* he is more brutal: in the only scene where he talks directly about his aspiration for artistic and ethical heights, his wish to mingle into the concepts of Truth–Goodness–Beauty, etc., he does it through the kitschy mode of representation; outdoing all his earlier efforts and then acknowledging that this path is doomed to a fall. The epilogue segment has always been read as separation, but I am inclined to read it also as an ultimate admission of defeat, the declaration that Trimurtis and Natarajas *will* fall. He is helpless; Rita, the representation of 'the other', is incapable of saving him. After this nightmarish dream, and after a series of violent scenes will come the final defeat: the promise to become like his father at the end of a period of penance; after a story in which Rita does save him but saves him only for this final defeat.

And in the absence of that metaphysical transcendence that he had been seeking, his 'art' turns into melodrama. Noticeably the section kept apart for the father had ended in melodrama and the switchover to an entirely different mode in the beginning of the childhood section comes as a real surprise at a first viewing of the film. With the youth section comes another mode, a mix of the Chaplinesque, of his own brand of humour, and of the gangster, and his brand of romantic realism. As the dream ends we see the return of pure melodrama.

PURSUITS OF
WHITENESS AND RICHES

What is this world of Rita and Raghunath that Raj would like to belong to? Why is Rita shown so often in relation to Raghunath? Why is her own father such a peripheral figure in the film? Could he not have provided that opposition to the hero, so crucial to a drama? Why did Raghunath have to occupy that position? And then, why is he so possessive of his ward? What is this peculiar bond between the two?

If we take a quick look back at the character of Rita we will find two sequences devoted to her childhood: in one she buys chocolates and talks of parties, the second is the party itself. When we first see her as a grown-up woman she, once again, is buying something in a shop. In the first frame containing her, in long shot (LS), she is not recognizable: we see only a woman in a white sari, with a string purse, inside a shop, framed beside the bust of a half-clad female mannequin. In the next shot the camera closes in on the string purse ('vanity bag' in the parlance of those days). In the third shot she emerges from the shop and only then do we see that it is Nargis and hence, the heroine of the film. So once again we see her associated with motifs of money and consumerism. Except for the sequences when she is with Raj, engaged in 'love' or engaged in fighting a legal battle for him, Rita is surrounded by such motifs of riches and luxe. Twice we see her sit down for dinner with Raghunath. They sit at either end of a banquet table: these scenes are highlighted by liveried attendants, frames composed with fruit-bowls, piled high with fruits, in the foreground. In both the sequences, the dinner is metaphorized (metonymically)[1] by their 'correct' way of eating soup. Rita turns the soup-spoon away from her, to let the soup fall off the spoon, as a 'show' of her state of mind. Before sitting down she has changed into her dressing gown, she has helped Raghunath to change into his. The issue of Westernization dominates this sequence containing the man and his ward. Commonly, Rita and Raghunath will be called 'Westernized people'—commonly, Raj has been called 'the common man's hero'.

The relationship that we observe between Rita and Raghunath is one that arises out of and is situated in a world of consumerism and Westernization. The disappearance of Rita's father makes more sense in this context, for Rita and Raghunath must be made to live together in this world, where Raj must enter, be seduced and then give up his ways and desire, to *belong*.

Once this logic is grasped it also becomes visible how despite all the coincidences, exaggerations and break in continuity-logic, popular cinema still conveys the feeling of an overall unity (though its audience might not be consciously perceiving this mechanism).

Rita and Raghunath are considerably different. He has a feudal background, and is a patriarch. But if we recall that he is one of those who pour money into the city of Bombay then Rita is a vehicle of its consumption. Later Raghunath is to buy a diamond necklace for her twenty-first birthday. In the party sequence Rita comes down in a flush of ornaments—in her ears, wrist, hair, matching the diamond necklace which is soon to adorn her bare neck. As she descends, the focus pans on to Raghunath (or cuts back to him) gazing at her admiringly and lovingly: he is framed against a laden buffet table and bottles of 'foreign' (bilayti) drinks (a little earlier he has poured out a drink to a guest).

It would be worthwhile to trace the history of the recurrence of the issue of rising consumerism and the spirit of consumption; and all that, in association with the issue of Westernization.

In *Aag*, Kewal goes to the city of Bombay and is desperate for work when he is picked up by a decadent artist, a landlord from some village who has come to the city to become a patron of the arts. He makes Kewal the director of his theatre company, lying closed now for the past few years. He reassures Kewal that money will not be a problem, 'I will spend

all my land money for your theatre.' Not simply 'all
my money' but 'all my land money.' Another film that
goes into many details concerning money, its source,
the nature of money and the consumption of money is
Mehboob's *Andaaz*. Both Nina (Nargis) and Raj (Raj
Kapoor) belong to families of feudal overlords. When
the film begins Raj is already in England, gone there
for 'higher studies', while Nina, with her father, is in
Shimla, riding horses, playing tennis and dancing in
clubs. Dilip (Dilip Kumar) is a nouveau riche, whose
family has made money in Africa. Nina and Raj marry
but stay on in Shimla playing golf. Nina does not want
to go to Bombay and face Dilip's love for her (and
hers for his), while Dilip, now made the director of
her father's estate (for he is now dead) looks after the
property, multiplying it and occasionally channelizing
some of it to charitable institutions or hospitals. After
spending three years of her married life in Shimla, Nina
returns to Bombay with Raj and a baby daughter. The
daughter has a birthday celebration—a party. Nina
sings a song, that suddenly breaks into the following
description:

> Here they dance, butler and bearer,
> Here dances the fat Ayah,
> Dari dara, dari dara, dari dara . . .
> There dances the hat of the black sahib,
> There dances the shadow of the fair *mem*.
> O my darling daughter, you are the queen of the stars.

The issue of consumerism and Westernization rises in these films not only out of thematic considerations but also from the consumeristic nature of the medium itself. While the pleasure elements implicit in consumerism and Westernization are linked with the characters of these films (the women in particular), they themselves fall victims to the problematic by becoming objects of pleasure.

Rita in *Awāra* and Nina in *Andaaz* are both motherless women. Had they been shown with their mothers, a separate line of argument would have opened up. They would have been in continuation with a feminine tradition or in opposition to it. But these women are shown as new women continuing the father's tradition instead: continuing the feudal and bringing it to the capitalistic. Nina in *Andaaz* hardly shows any direct interest in her business, passing on all responsibilities to Dilip (the story too revolves more on the interrelationships now), whereas Rita is a legal person belonging to an institution intricately connected with the post-industrial capitalistic mode, thematically bonded with the character of Raghunath.

The bond between Rita and Raghunath is demonstrated in a manner that would call for more psychoanalytical explanation; for the relationship between Raghunath and his ward, Rita, is shown as something more than a father-daughter relationship. We will go over a few sequences and then come back to this question.

Raj and Rita have united after twelve years; we see them under the photograph of the child Rita. Raj takes her sari-end and ties it around his fingers in a symbolic gesture; a romantic music piece grows louder on the sound track. Normally at this point the popular cinema would bring in a song/and or dance picturization on the couple. In this case, the music does change to a song by Rita; but she has now left Raj and has returned home. The song begins with Rita entering her house. She sings, 'Ever since my lover has returned, my heart has been beating wild.' She runs around the house, arranges some flowers and then goes up to her room to change into her 'dressing gown'. Hardly has the refrain 'Ever since my lover has returned' died down, when the front door opens and Raghunath enters through the door, in a top-angle shot (in her point-of-view). Incidentally, Karmakar says that he was aware of this slant in the guardian-ward relationship and was asked to compose the shots accordingly; but he had never heard Abbas and Kapoor discuss why they had conceived of this rather unusual relationship. V.P. Sathe insisted that Abbas and he wanted to establish that 'Raghunath was a little bit in love with Rita, he admired her, but she considered him only as a father figure.' Asked why it had to be so, his reply was, 'Many older men do fall in love with women younger to them. Besides both of them were very alike, they shared the same profession.'

Rita runs down to greet Raghunath, scolding him for being late for dinner, and asks an attendant to fetch his dressing gown. In a shot, very similar to the one between Leela and Raghunath, now Rita stands with the gown, Raghunath turns round to face her. And just when in the earlier sequence, Raghunath had embraced Leela, here the shot cuts to a close-up of a clock. Karmakar confirms that Kapoor had intended to relate the two sequences.

Seated at the dining table, Raghunath shows apprehension at her re-union with her childhood sweetheart, 'What if he takes away something very precious from this house . . .' In the second dining sequence, Rita has just returned from the beach—Raghunath tries to speak of his responsibilities for a ward and gives himself away, 'I had promised your father that if any boy should . . . or if you like some boy, then he should pass my scrutiny.' He cannot bring himself to even utter the word 'love', and say—'if any boy should love you . . .' His fear of loss, his reaction to the whole matter is of interest because of its intensity. Rita has become 'a precious object' to Raghunath, he possesses her: their relationship is of possession and wealth. Wealth is wealth, for it is possessed. Thus, though Rita is a wealthy woman herself and a professional woman, there is no question of her walking out to do as she pleases. Once again we realize that it is not a simple tale of generational conflict. Raghunath and Rita are *one*, they belong together, together they help perpetuate the system, and Raj must come and *belong* to that system. The visible conflict between them belongs to the level of the tale/ story while at the argument or proposition level they are one.

There is one sequence which is very strange and stands quite apart from the diegetic level (the level of the tale) of the film. It follows the song by Rita which at first seems redundant (i.e., it will not harm the narrative at all if the song is removed). Rita sings a 'song of separation' (a viraha-song) on her terrace, 'Come! My desires writhe in pain and the night is about to end.' She is in her sleeping robes and as the song ends she goes and falls asleep on her bed. Meanwhile, in parallel cutting, Raj climbs a water-pipe and Raghunath (in his dressing gown) goes up the stairs (both the series of images in ELS): both wanting to go to her. As her head touches the pillow and she is seen falling asleep, a hand enters the frame. It could be any one of the males and there are a few seconds of attempt from the director to create this confusion, till Raj enters the frame. A little later Raghunath knocks on the door, driving Raj to hide. Raghunath enters to show her the invitation cards for the party—at this point of the night? Rita asks him meaningfully, 'Can I invite all my friends?' Raghunath, making it clear that he has understood her, says with an emphasis, 'Yes, *all* your friends.' The scene ends here, without going back to Raj.

Just as some very obvious psychoanalytical explanations can be attached to the dream scene, so can the relationship of Rita and Raghunath be seen as an Oedipal (or Electral) situation, so that the woman must break out of this, towards greater maturity: which Rita does eventually. And the film can be seen as the story of the Oedipal conflict in its various manifestations. But I feel that that is not enough; I feel that to do so would be to explain away the film. Recognition of codes, motifs or references and their analysis is one matter, but this way of reading alone is not fully satisfying. Sexual allegories on the other hand speak of a history of complexities that carry certain historical moments.

Indian cinema very often brings in a father–daughter question (American cinema does it too and Stanley Cavell has remarked on it in his *Pursuits of Happiness*). It was quite a running theme in the films of Ritwik Ghatak, where the incestuous 'angle' touched upon the brother–sister relationship. In *Meghe Dhaka Tara*, Nita and Shankar are composed in greater harmony than she is with her fiancé. In Ghatak's *Suvarnarekha*, Ishwar, elder brother of the heroine Seeta and old enough to be her father, had never married and looked after Seeta all along. When he thinks of marrying late, Seeta appeases him by whispering into his ears, 'I am your mother,' leaving him to plead with her, 'Then don't leave me the way our mother had.'[2] I have talked of the motherless heroines of the popular cinema; of Nina in *Andaaz*, who has a breakdown when her father dies and no man ever after can really make her as happy as she had been with her father.

A woman's 'problem' with the father and its resolution can very well be read as a sign of the attainment of adulthood in the modern sense of the term; which means I am returning to the Freudian explanation of such motifs. Yet, once again, I would suggest that there is more to it than the question of maturity or adjustment. It is in fact a mature bond. All the father–daughter (or brother–sister) relationships portrayed in these films are mature, adult relationships. What is new in these films is that they speak of daughters continuing the patriarchal order instead of sons. Maybe one can go back into the Indian genesis myths, particularly to the story of Brahma who desired his daughter Gayatri to bring the human race into being, or to mythological traces of a supreme father's primitive desire to unite with the daughter to create a 'purer' race when the race as it existed was imperiled, or an expression in its turn of the even more extensive primitive desire to break a primitive taboo, to break free from a racial or civilizational crisis—a desire that surfaces, for example, in Werner Herzog's film *Aguirre, the Wrath of God* (where the crisis was of course a creation of Aguirre and his acute megalomania, but that in turn spoke of man's inherent lust for power and probed into the history of cruelty). It is a great pity that there is no way of knowing what Kapoor and Abbas were thinking when they filled the film with the break of a taboo, which is a rare topic for Indian cinema.

Another very important example of this 'special relationship' is the sequence in which Raj attempts to kill Raghunath, a sequence that has been discussed earlier: Raj does not listen to Rita's plea, but Raghunath does. Rita stops him as he is about to stab Raj. Rita says, 'Have you gone crazy too?' Raghunath checks himself and says, 'I had, for a little while.' He comes back to reason and sanity at *her* words.

There is enough evidence to show that Kapoor was conscious of this 'special' relationship between these two characters, of the split of the character of Rita into a figure of idealization and a symbol of pleasure. It is not possible to know what was behind this consciousness. Some would hold that it is not important to know the intentions of an author; some others are of the opinion that authors hardly 'intend' anything and in this case Kapoor is only following some 'formula way' and his money-making instincts. I would, however, like to figure out what might have been in an author's mind, trying to be in his shoes; I would like to ignore him, at other times, and place him in the context of his time and tradition; I would also like to occasionally put aside the above two modes and 'see' things as years of studies and teaching have taught me to. I have tried to follow all three ways into the study of this film.

THE PHOTOGRAPH

We have referred already to the use director Kapoor makes of Rita's childhood photograph. We come back in this chapter to the photograph once again to illustrate how through repeated use a visual motif accumulates meanings around it till it becomes a symbol, or how an icon undergoes a process of signification to turn into a symbol.

The first time we are made aware of the importance of the photograph is when Raj turns it upside down to go out on a thieving assignment; and the photograph is no longer just a reminder of a childhood friendship but the guardian of his conscience. In an earlier sequence—the childhood sequence—we have already seen the photograph, as child Raj hangs it up on the wall after Rita's disappearance. The child draws his mother's (and our) attention to it, as he asks: 'Isn't Rita's photograph very beautiful?'

The third use of the photograph for the purpose of 'bracketing' in the vice-den sequence has been mentioned in a previous chapter. The dance of the vice-den moll represents the temptation in the way of the hero and identifies it as all other temptations lying before him. Destiny brings a hero to a particular adverse situation, but it is for the hero to decide for himself whether he can rise above it or would succumb to it. The moll spreads out the invitation through the song, 'Come, the season is ripe.' The hero spurns the invitation, for he carries within him an ideal. The photograph is an iconic representation of that ideal. The first dissolve registers a transition from that ideal to a more ambivalent space, where the fall of the hero can take place. The second dissolve draws him out of that ambiance; back to the security/sustenance of the ideal represented by the photograph. The portion bracketed off loses its 'power' as it is bracketed out by the more powerful image, which will keep recurring at crucial points in the narrative and through the plot line.

Raj visits the house of the adult Rita and through another photograph *recognizes* her. He wants her to meet his mother, who had been, so to say, guarding his memory of her, wiping the photograph with the end of her sari. But this event, i.e., the reunion of the two women, is not shown. A shot transition joins the couple situated at one space beside one photograph to another space, where again they are standing under a similar photograph. Through the shift in space the shift is from ignorance to knowledge (both had been ignorant of the other's identity); from a state of loss to a state of gain (both now love each other); from a state of separation to a state of union (separation and union being phases in the development of love). Separation and union is the 'real story' the film is telling us; and the story (as we understand stories to be) is a vehicle for the relating of that 'other story'. We are in the habit of cribbing about the absence of logic in films. Only because we try to find logic where there is none. With this logic Rita's being in total love at this moment seems ridiculous since she has never been shown waiting for Raj. But love being an a priori, a 'given' for both the parties concerned, a single photograph is sufficient to take the film from the topic of loss to that of gain. Rita says, 'Where were you lost, Raj?' Raj replies 'In search of you.' It is the male whose story is being told in this male cinema; with the woman as the female 'other'. It is a story of union, loss, separation, and reunion where it is the male who is to be united, to be separated, etc. So at the narrative level the photograph helps in the recognition and reunion of the characters, but at the level of signification the two characters stand at that 'framed idealism' and begin an adult relationship from a perfected position; from a state of full acceptance and love. (In a realistic mode such a sudden jump would be totally unacceptable and the author-filmmaker would be required to show the mechanics of courtship or getting into love or whatever.)

The fifth use of the photograph is before the birthday party when the camera trolleys in towards the photograph, as the child Rita's words come on the voice-over. He remembers his promise to her that he would buy expensive gifts for her when he grew up, though Rita had then said, 'Is it only bought things that make a gift?' As Raj had ignored that piece of idealism from the 'ideal girl', the transition is to be the giving of the ideal gift through the procurement of the non-ideal gilt. For this he confronts both the father figures. Jugga reminds him that the price of belonging to the class of the shareefs is high (he cannot belong there by the gift of a flower).

Raghunath advises him to 'look carefully' as he walks his path. We can see that the shift from the photograph to the representation of the woman in the party, as 'the jolly good fellow', the two small sections with Jugga and Raghunath, are filled with sentences with double meanings. The question of the gift shifts from an offering of love to an offering made to a particular world to gain admission into it. Rita and Raghunath belong to a world which will now be represented through motifs such as Rita's black dress (the only time she wears it in the film), piano, cake, tinsels, and now this new addition of the diamond necklace.

But the first of the more remarkable uses of the photograph (and the sixth in the chronology of uses) comes in the scene where Raj kills the man on the street (or maybe strangulates him to unconsciousness). From his kneeling position Raj looks up aghast and confounded at his own act. He seems to be looking for something to hold on to, something to extricate himself out of the situation. Shouldn't he be thinking at this point of the flesh and blood woman he loves? No, his conscience has always been answerable to 'an ideal love'. A long dissolve of the photograph appears over his face, to show his inner state and the response from within to his cry of help.

The photograph now connects the murder theme. In this seventh use, the photograph appears in the shack where Raj is now staying with his mother. Jugga is strangulated under the photograph.

The most elaborate use of the photograph is associated with the sequence in which Raj attempts to kill Raghunath. The photograph actually appears quite early in the sequence when Raghunath comes out of his study to talk to Rita. Or perhaps we should go back even earlier, to the sequence where the judge is in his study and is framed by two photographs of Rita on either side, both recent photographs; in one she is in a sari, while in the other she is in her lawyer's black gown. It is the photographs of the adult woman that adorn his walls. This is the sequence in which Raj comes to meet the older man and they come to clashes once again.

In the sequence in which Raj attacks Raghunath, the childhood photograph is reintroduced as soon as the judge comes out of his study to meet Rita in a section of the house not shown earlier. As the two get into a conversation and as the shots change the photograph is always there in the background. On close inspection one notices that the photograph is readjusted each time the camera angle and distance are changed—to ensure the right composition.

Raj enters, knife in hand, through the window. Rita shrieks, rushes to him and pleads, 'Have you gone crazy?' Her lover does not glance once at her and pushes her aside instead. He raises his hand to strike at the judge; strikes at the glass of the photograph cracking and shattering it. Raj looks up, sees the face in the photograph and freezes. Raghunath jeers at him, 'What, have you taken a scare?' The young man keeps silent for a while before he answers, 'Be thankful to the one who has saved your life.' In this final use of the photograph the representation and the represented are split apart. The adult woman is not the woman who can curb his urge to kill, The 'ideal woman' in the framed representation is the child Rita. Both the child and the woman share the same iconography of party, cake and all the baubles that money can buy.

The scene ends as Raghunath in his turn picks up the knife to strike at Raj and Rita repeats the previous sentence. 'Have you gone crazy too?' Raghunath is checked by the woman for they share a certain empathy, certain commonalities and the same world. He murmurs, 'I had, for a little while.'

Kapoor has always been troubled with the question of the representation of woman. *Aag* illustrates

more than amply how he could never bring about
a reconciliation between physical human love and
passions and the other passions of creativity and
spirituality. For him, in *Aag* the childhood love for a
girl was ideal—it was associated with the promise of
the staging of *Vilwamangal*. But of course she does
not become the perfect/ideal representation. She is
taken away by her parents and thus is removed from
the screen. When Nargis becomes the heroine of his
theatrical company in the city, what he does with
her on the stage, i.e., her representation thereafter,
is what constitutes pleasurable, consumable kitsch.
Her performance, her singing, draws praise from the
artist friend, who 'paints the body', but Kewal (Raj
Kapoor) tells her that her act lacks soul. He asks her
repeatedly to try hard, to try and reach for the skies.
Throughout the film his refrain is, 'I want to take
theatre to transcendental heights!' But he cannot—not
in the film. He is appalled when he learns that Nargis
loves him and realizes his own feelings for her. He
burns his face in fear and shame. At the end of *Aag* Raj
Kapoor is reunited with his childhood sweetheart who
he finds as his legitimate life-partner, but the ultimate
legitimacy comes from the promise that he will stage
Vilwamangal and she will be his Chintamani.

The film *Awāra* never projects clearly the ideal
for the representation of women; what is *not* ideal
is spelt out very clearly. The framed representation
thus becomes an index of that vague yearning for an

ideal state whereas the representation through real-life artistes (one of them a star) becomes the vehicle for conveying all his darker thoughts and misgivings.

Towards the end of the film the photograph is shattered, never to appear again. The film ends with the promise that Raj will join the world of Rita and Raghunath after undergoing a period of penance and achieve the legitimacy that he has been seeking all along.

MUSIC IN AWĀRA: SONG AND DANCE PICTURIZATION

The special status of music in Indian cinema, the importance given to song and dance picturization, the popularity of film songs as a phenomenon independent of the popularity of films they occur in, are some of the reasons why a separate chapter should be devoted to this topic. There is no need to explore the reasons behind the occurrence of music—songs and dance— and so much of it—in our cinema. We could very well take it as a well-established feature of the Indian film. If it 'works' for its audience, then it is for me to show how the filmmaker has attempted to make it work in his film; how the song and dance picturization does not fragment the film but in fact contributes to the total experience of the film instead.

The decade of the fifties was a watershed for Indian film music, and the music in *Awāra* bears the marks of the period. The most important things to happen in this decade were the end of a singing style, the introduction of Western music in a big way, and improved recording facilities (the introduction of the condenser microphone). The traditional singing style till then had an open, full-throated quality to it, with very little delicate ornamentation of the voice that was sharply projected outwards. The death of Kundan Lal Saigal can be taken as an event that marks the end of an era. The new singing style, Bhaskar Chandavarkar explains, had a crooning intimate quality; the singers brought in more depth, modulation and perspective to their voice. Kapoor makes total utilization of this style to go with the chiaroscuro lighting and numerous close-ups. One very important reason behind the popularity of this film, for its love and romance, is the effect achieved by the juxtaposition of close-ups in various compositions and dialogues delivered in many shades of whispers.

Chandavarkar, basing himself on information gathered from sound recordist Minoo Katrak, whom he holds in great regard, tells me how the sound recording was done under primitive conditions in what was practically a godown, but glorified beyond all proportions to be described as the sound studio of the Famous Laboratory at Tardeo. There was an abandoned, but covered well that produced a resonance which Katrak used to his advantage, which, in turn, he highlighted (or reduced) by other means. This was before the time of electronic treatment of the music or the multi-track recording system. It strikes one with awe even to think how the wide range of pitch, timbre, and the resonances of various instruments, voices, noises were all balanced in this primitive set-up. Katrak did all the song-recordings for the film, while the sound in general was handled by Allauddin, a lifelong associate of Kapoor.

This was also the period when the influence of the Bengali schools of music had receded and the influence of UP folk was at its highest; second in line was the steadily growing influence of Western music. Kapoor had used Ram Ganguly in *Aag,* and the music of that film was naturally very nearly all Bengali. He had brought in the duo Shanker–Jaikishan in *Barsaat* and had also introduced his signature tune from 'Waves of the Danube' in that film (snatches of it can be heard in nearly all his films till *Mera Naam Joker).* Both in *Barsaat* and in *Awāra,* Kapoor and his music directors retain some of the older styles of music as well; in both films they use Shamshad Begum as the representative of that era. But what is new in *Awāra* is the introduction of the choral mode of singing—a borrowal from the Indian People's Theatre Association (IPTA) style.

He also goes in for other modes that will remain his favourites till the end, e.g., Goan folk songs, obtained through his assistant music director Sunny Castellino; or Russian folk songs (perhaps obtained from friends in the IPTA). It is interesting to note that just as in the case of film style so in the case of music, Kapoor brings together so many styles (ranging from Western and Indian classical, to the various folk styles, to what by now is clearly 'filmy', to the IPTA choral, etc.), yet the overall experience is unified and pleasing, often even exhilarating.

This mélange is no sign of ignorance or callousness or indifference to perfection; nor does it mean that since Kapoor was associating with Abbas, hence the IPTA music, or since he has Castellino in his team, hence there is the Goan folk song. As will be somewhat clear from the study below, as well as through the study of the film itself, Kapoor is meticulous and self-exacting. He was a musical person himself and played several musical instruments. It is reported that he often composed the opening notes of a song and then gave it to the music director. So this mélange is intentional; partly, it would seem, in keeping with the general 'ambivalence' of the work as a whole and partly because he is thinking many thoughts. It should be noted that one cannot find such a crowding of musical motifs in his earlier *Barsaat*. He is striving towards a contemporaneity, a connection with certain ideology-based, cultural reforms and practices; he is also trying to make 'popular cinema', which he has inherited from his father, more 'meaningful' to himself and he is obsessed with the desire to 'reach the masses'. We will now try and see how he employs these diverse elements and find some reasons behind their success.

The title music of *Awāra* is divided into two sections: one expressing the topic of 'transcendental heights' and the other the entire 'Awāra boon' song, played at a fast rhythm The title song, or the film itself, begins with the chant of 'Namah Shivaya' accompanied with temple bells and flute. The chant gives way to a small piece of folk melody on the piano-accordion and a few snatches of music from all over the film, lastly giving way to the tune of the theme song played on a mandolin accompanied by a chorus. Both the piano accordion and the mandolin are primarily folk instruments. Thus we find the division of the classical and the popular made manifest, characteristically caught in a close relationship.

We have noted already the use of the theatrical way of announcing characters. As Raghunath enters the court, a trumpet sounds a fanfare, giving him a grand entry. All the Raghunath sections contain trumpet pieces or the rumbling of percussions, while most smaller motifs associated with the Raj-sections contain the flute and the sitar. One departure from this is made for the depiction of Raghunath's love, when a romantic piece, very similar to that played during Raj's first meeting with Rita in their adulthood, accompanies the sequence; interestingly, the piece is from the previous film Barsaat.

The Raghunath section, has two songs; both sung by representatives of the marginal sections of society, and both in chorus. The use of the chorus here draws on the IPTA influence and moves away from it. Group singing or the chorus as voice of protest, as means of achieving equality of existence, and as a neutralizing power, is something that has been picked up by contemporary political movements or cult groups. Boatmen or city migrants singing in groups, however, has been a common thing in theatre and cinema. But here in *Awāra* the group singing is further emphasized by a female chorus, attaching further political connotations. The putting together of the traditional 'Hai Allah' and the modern chorus is something drawn from the IPTA, something very much of a novelty at the time.

The picturization of the song too is significant. The boatmen song has been shot in the Soviet montage style. Backlighting without any front key lights throw the figure of the lead singer into darkness; and his dark form, looming over the camera, cuts the screen into various graphic shapes. The sequence is composed by juxtaposing shots in which image size and the inner dynamics of the movements alternate. If in one the shot movement is from left to right and the image size big, in the next shot the movement is from right to left and the figures tiny. Single figures alternate with the group. If in a shot the group occupy the upper edge of the frame, in the next shot they are likely to form an ant-chain at the bottom of the frame. In alternate shots two different diagonals cut across the frame. The song begins with Raghunath's gunshot and continues well into the next sequence where dialogues are foregrounded and the chorus, with a slightly changed humming of the melody, extends till Leela asks about the song.

The migrant-labourer song or the Seeta-song begins with a female chorus, and seems like a voice-over (as narrator's voice—this has been commented upon earlier); when the labourers appear on the screen the female chorus is lifted off, and with the source now identified on screen, the voice-over gives *way* to the incidental. Again when Leela is thrown out on the roads the chorus is back. The source of the song is Bihari folk song and the special percussion used is typical of this music. The common allegation that popular film songs are composed as separate entities and are simply added almost anywhere in a film may hold good in many cases, but it is sad when we take no note of exemplary efforts. This sequence, coming at the end of the high style adopted for Raghunath, and before the realistic mode of the childhood sequence immediately afterwards, is in low contrast 'natural' lighting. The song closes with a striking evidence of the superior craftsmanship of the sound recordists who mix several sounds on the soundtrack, e.g., rain-sound, the cry of an infant, the female chorus, the musical instruments, and later the voice of Jugga.

The boot-polish song is a fraction of a complete song, recorded to be included in the album, but used partially. It is a chorus all through. Though Raj alone, among the children in his class, polishes shoes to pay for his fees, the image of the child Raj at work is superimposed over the classroom image, and a group of children sing the song. The song begins with the melody of a Boy Scout song.[1] The song is not lip-synched. The tendency towards generalization evident throughout the film is obvious here too. The word 'matwala' echoes the word 'awāra'. Thus, Shailendra and Kapoor suggest the nature of work available to and typical of an awāra: it is unorganized work, away from the system of capitalism. It is important to note (and we tend to overlook this while talking about the gift motif in *Awāra)* that this is the only time Raj buys something with money earned through labour and buys a gift for Rita. This gift however does not reach Rita. Later a stolen diamond necklace will adorn the lady-in-black.

The songs hereafter (except in the dream sequence) are sung either by the hero or the heroine and these have no chorus accompaniment: they are songs associated with an individualistic hero and his heroine.

The first song of Raj, '*Main awāra boon*' brings out all the ambivalences and clashes of dialectics: yet the song is a foot-tapping number. Raj is a people's man, impersonating the tramp and at the same time picking people's pockets. The lyrics are the cry of a 'sad heart full of love', 'I have no home, no family, but I sing the song of love', he sings 'I am the victim of destiny and of your love.' The Chaplinesque act, the silent cinema quote, the kitschy image of dancing fisherwomen on a truck, the realism of naked dark poor babies or

women washing utensils at a tap—all combine in the
visual. The melody is gay, based on the raag *Bhairavi*
(it also resembles gypsy music, which might explain its
popularity in the erstwhile Soviet Union, especially in
the central Asian Republics.) The instruments used are
the mandolin and the piano-accordion.

As a contrast, the vice-den song uses muted trumpet,
oboe and castanets, and is in the style of Latin American
music in keeping with the sequence. The lyric should be
of interest today, for it begins with the numerals 'One,
two, three'. The disappearance of poetry in film songs
is a widely discussed theme these days. This song of the
vamp already prefigures that phenomenon, though the
purpose here is quite obviously derisive.

Chandavarkar drew my attention to a very
interesting use of a Russian folk song melody in the
sequence where the police car chases Raj running away
from the police with a stolen car. Later in the same
scene, while 'pretending' to tune a piano, Raj hums
another recognizable Russian folk tune. But when Raj
recognizes Rita, the mood is romantic, the music used
is a piece on sitar and flute. This piece is the same as
the one used for Raj's 'first' look at Rita's photograph
after his release and is used a couple of times for other
sequences with the same mood.

The first song on Rita is based on a Punjabi folk
song highlighted by the use of the dholak as percussion
accompaniment. Lata Mangeshkar sings the song in
the traditional manner. It is curious that the song that

ends with the entry of Raghunath and establishes his closeness to Rita uses this traditional mode.

The beach episode creates a romantic mood by the use of a popular Goan folk melody. Kapoor's predilection for inter-textuality in his films, mentioned earlier, is manifested here: for this song later becomes a very famous and full-fledged song in *Bobby*. Jumping chronology, let me mention that the piece used after the sequence of Leela's death will yield yet another famous song 'O *Basanti pawan paagal* in *Jis Desh Mein Ganga Behti Hai*.

A piece of intense music matches the mood of the sequence on the beach, supporting Raj's dark passions and violence. As the changes of mood are sudden in this three-part love-scene so the music covers so many styles—one can only remark on the fact that 'it works'.

The boat-song unites, finally, Western and Indian musical forms and instruments kept separate until now. The song is based on the raag *Gara-Kaafi*, using both minor and major chords. The eroticism of the sequence is carried even independently by the song accounting for its popularity. The singers employ the intimate crooning style. The tempo is slow; the *theka, chaal* and *jhonka,* the song (i.e., the modulation and the manner in which the word syllables meet the beat) all contribute towards the seductive appeal of the song matching the images and the cutting patterns adopted here. Extremely effective is the combination of the many monosyllabic words (the two-syllable words employed are broken in halves) sung in staccato manner, each syllable to each smaller beat division. Then a long vowel-end flows over two beats, with an 'empty' division at regular intervals.

(slip)	(beat)	(beat)	(beat)	(empty)
Dum	bharjo	udharmuh	phere	
X	X	X	0	
O	chanda	a	a	
X	X	X	0	
Main	unsé	pyār	kar	lungi
X	X	X	0	
Baa	ten	hajaar	kar	lungi
X	X	X	0	

The composition of the visuals plays with the actors in stasis and movement making use of the fact that the entire song was to be picturized in the narrow confines of a dinghy. The lighting is extremely efficient, with variations of key lighting, fillers, rim-lighting and of course backlighting. During the first stanza the actors do not move; the camera cuts to a high (when Rita stands hugging the pole) or a low (when she sits with Raj or he sings alone) position, choosing different angles. The entire second stanza is composed in three shots. The camera, cutting on the same axis, changes camera distance very slightly and every cut is on matched movement and very gradually the camera closes in. In the next verse the shots contain only one of the couple each. When the song ends, the two approach each other in the reflection in the water. (Karmakar talks of Kapoor's passion for perfection: an entire day's shooting was abandoned after having exposed a can, to get the stanzas (1) and (2) right.)

Chandavarkar considers the dream sequence composition the ultimate triumph of the craft of Shankar-Jaikishen. Several small pieces accompany the three principal songs. A small piece, accompanied by temple bells, is played along with the prelude images. There is a chorus and another fast piece on the xylophone. Then the tempo changes and the song begins in halting, fragmented fashion, ending in a tremulous continuity of 'Aa ja' The song is interrupted abruptly and the second piece begins with the anguished cry of Raj, sung by Manna Dey. The crooning style of Mukesh is abandoned this one time. One is struck with awe to think how the recording of this piece was achieved: Raj's cry, the yell of the group dancers, the simulated sound of leaping flames, and the several instrumental pieces are all orchestrated together with remarkable expertise. The song begins in a feet-stamping marching song fashion. The fist raising slogan of This is not life' is matched by the leaping flames. As Raj climbs up the hills the chant 'Namah Shivaya' takes over. The third song begins with another small piece accompanied on the mandolin. There is one more end-piece that gives way to Raj's cry "Rita!' Of course the above description can hardly explain why the entire musical score has worked so well; it only serves to demonstrate the amount of work that has gone into it.

The two songs by Raj and Rita, though separated by the party song, will be taken up together as they resemble each other in tempo and melody. Rita's song of yearning begins with a piano piece but gives way to Indian instruments. The words flow lightly over the beat divisions, touching the sound portion of the beat lightly. The song seems quite redundant until the 'incest' aspect of the sequence becomes clear.

Raj's song on the beach is an achievement of teamwork, of composition, editing, singing, lighting, etc. Kapoor used to refer to Mukesh as his 'soul'. Mukesh gives the scene and the song what is expected of him. His slightly 'nasal' voice that did not always touch upon the notes squarely (a mode of 'imperfection' that folk singing often flaunts) lay behind his tremendous popular appeal. This was the people's song and not 'song sung by professionals'. It also had a conversational property in the manner of Saigal. (Mukesh in fact can be said to have filled in many ways the vacuum left by Saigal.) The song here is again in slow tempo but unlike in Rita's song the consonants are emphasized and they hit upon the sound part of the beat. The significant feature of the visual is that Raj moves continuously towards the audience. Once again there is a play between movement and stasis. In the static shots which are held for long durations, there is very little movement within the frame. Raj's movements are not rhythmic, they have the look of natural movement. But occasionally, as in the case of the knife coming from off-screen and getting embedded on the trunk to a perfectly matching beat (or a couple of cuts on beat), the matched rhythm of movement and song produce the subtle but desired mood. Occasionally, Raj, from an in-screen gaze, takes a gaze off-screen in a slow movement of his head (making 15°-45° angles with the camera). The mood lighting and the breeze playing with his hair add up to an image of desire. It is Raj again who looks offscreen in the boat sequence, while Rita is made to look all along towards him. A lot of the visual pleasure in Indian cinema is generated by or is made to revolve around the male stars.

This song can be restrained entirely within the narrative and at the same time can be taken as a direct appeal at the audience. The double meaning of the words perhaps is not lost on the audience, as the words come from a performer to his audience. The song is also a filmography (three films old) of Kapoor and that way the song is also coming from the filmmaker: 'Loving you, my friend, I only laughed, I only cried' (with its reference to the two performing masks of *Aag,* and the masks as logo on the credit cards of *Mera Naam Joker*: the laughing and the crying faces of a performer).

My heart burned and turned to *Fire*
Tears flowed and *Rains* came down.

I was an Awāra, like those clouds,
And I laughed and I cried.

An oboe and a base-flute support the voice. After the song Rita joins him and the intensely passionate sequence is then supported by the raag *Darbari* played on the flute.

The accordion appears in a close-up now in the party sequence. The satiric, ambivalent aspect of *Awāra* permeates every element of the film. The musician presses upon the keys with a flourish and he sings away with a gay 'He is a jolly good fellow', as Rita, bejewelled, in a black rich off-shouldered dress, descends the grand staircase. Because of 'the jolly good fellow' and her likes Raj must leave in disgrace. Another jolly song is picked up by Rita's Eurasian friend (remember the other one in the first party sequence and the words, 'Rita, your father is calling you'). The song can be a Rita soliloquy (the reference to Kapoor's blue eyes in this black and white film is amusing), but if her discovery is shameful or painful to her, the song does not match her mood. The dancer looks towards the camera and twists and turns,

I've loved a traitor, I've looked into his eyes,
O God, what have I done?

As the film becomes more and more dramatic, the singing and dancing cease. All the instruments used now are Indian except for some drums and violin. Apart from an important composition at the time of Leela's death (mentioned earlier) the other significant one is an organ-piece with church bells that accompany the 'modern crucifixion' of the romantic hero. But as the prison gates close on the awāra and the key turns on the lock the lively music of '*Awāra hoon*' on mandolin and accordion fade in—as in the title cards—thus putting the closing arc of another bracket to the entire film.

THE NARRATIVE STRUCTURE

Under 'narrative structure', I propose the use of the flashback as the first point of interest and the entry point for a study of the formal and structural unity of *Awāra*. In most of the popular films where it is used, the flashback (FB) is a mere tool for explaining something in reference to the past or providing a piece of information without which the story cannot proceed. It is particularly common in suspense films, where the FB is used with great effectiveness to disclose a secret; to cause sudden twists and turns in the story or simply to divulge why the man in white shoes is out for the hero's blood! Unfortunately, like most narrative techniques or devices, this also has been taken for granted: it is there, either one uses it or one does not.

All stories begin at a certain point in time at a certain point in the life of the protagonist. At this point he is what he is because of his past, and his social and familial background. This past and this background must be established in the beginning of a narrative film.

One of the functions of the establishing sequence is to create the requisite stylistic ambiance for a particular film and to establish its genre, which in its turn will determine the flow of events, or the psychological make-up and motivation for certain actions of the hero or the heroine and others. For example, when in a Western, a town sheriff is ready to risk his life and performs heroic feats with ease and grace, then we do not seek explanation in his upbringing. Again, a hero with a haunted look is not a pathological case when he is part of the suspense genre that probes into the psychology of fear through the film. If in a melodrama, a woman is seen to be suffering silently and tearfully, then it is the genre that requires or uses a certain typology, and then her crying might not be a mark of moral weakness after all.

In other words, a filmmaker would take the same pains to endow a hero or a heroine with totally unbelievable predicates, to give the most blatantly illogical twists to events, to bring in the most fantastic coincidences, as another filmmaker would take to create characters and events and places in the closest correspondence with chosen reality. While the former makes the camera do 'things' in order to create a world which is conceptual, where a theme or an idea is to be played out, the latter seeks to reproduce a segment of the real world.

In genre cinema, the function of the FB is not limited to providing information or some specially desired effect; but is more often directed to that particular tampering with the time element, the sudden shift of space, the sudden jump in the character's age or behaviour that will make the theme flow in a particular way. These visual shifts create effects quite different from those produced by a FB in a novel. So though this narrative device comes to cinema from literature, it has a distinct identity in cinema.

The narrative illusionistic cinema strives towards a seamlessness to create an illusion of reality, and a FB is introduced in such a manner as to make it quick to comprehend. Usually, a dissolve is used to mark the transition from the present time to the past in the FB. In *Awāra* that is the way the FB is brought in the first time: through a dissolve. In the middle of the FB the film comes back to the present time for a few seconds, and again through a series of dissolves superimposed on an image the FB is resumed. The interesting thing about the FB in *Awāra* is that it has no fixed endpoint, as is usually brought about by another dissolve often going back to the image with which the FB had begun. The FB here is divided into the Raghunath section, the childhood section, and the adult section. We will describe the various modes of transition used between the sections before we come to discuss how the FB ends.

In the first section, Raghunath is being interrogated by Rita. She asks him about his past when he had abandoned his wife at a point when she was about to deliver her child. The camera trolleys in towards the older man from a mid-long shot (MLS), while she repeats her question insistently, 'Remember when, why and how you had abandoned your child.' The camera movement as a probe into his mind ends and holds him in a big close-up. The image blurs and dissolves on an image of the waters of the Ganga.

As a matter of fact, nearly the whole of the film is in FB as the memory of the father and not of the hero. Even when things are shown which he could not have known, they are still 'his memory', giving him, in the process, an added importance.

Once Raghunath has driven his wife out of his house, Leela is on the streets; Raj's birth is heralded by the cry of an infant. Jugga appears on the scene (the appearance of Jugga is also something which neither Raghunath nor Raj would have known about). Still, the film proceeds as it would have if the film was constructed in a linear fashion.

The childhood sequence is different stylistically; and more importantly, it is not part of Raghunath's memory in any way. The director seems to be aware of this point. Besides, he must announce the fact of migration, which is so crucial to this genre. So the film comes back to the courtroom where Rita is interrogating Raghunath, and over that image runs a series of dissolves of a train, the Victoria Terminus and the roads of Bombay with the state transport bus prominent in the image. The narration (mentioned in an earlier chapter) is quite specific: 'So your unfortunate wife had to leave Lucknow and your innocent child (children) began to be brought up in the slums of Bombay.'

Showing the child protagonist growing up into an adult is a favourite theme with filmmakers. For a heroine there could be the cliche of a bud blossoming into an open flower. For a hero it can be a game of football; the ball kicked high by the boy coming down to be received by the grown-up man. Cliche, or not, these visuals demonstrate the common predicates that establish the male–female difference. The logic of the mode of transition in this film is connected with its thematic preoccupation: the bread or roti that is to be earned and the related question as to how it should be earned by a common man. In a remand home the boys have queued up for their afternoon meal. Little Raj is given a roti, he looks at it silently for a while, and then bursts out laughing. The voice on the sound track is that of Raj Kapoor. The image cuts to the adult Raj in prison stripes laughing over a roti in hand. With the shift in time the mood of the film changes. The melodrama of the previous section, the accumulated adversities pursuing the little boy relentlessly, the boot-polish song with its appeal to the sympathies of the audience, the painful captivity and plight of children in orphanages or remand homes have been played out quickly and at one stroke the gloom is displaced.

The logical progression of an erring boy from a remand home to the prison is captured in this traditional sequence through which the child passes on to adulthood. I have mentioned earlier how the audience welcomes the star, in the prison pyjamas, holding a stale half burnt roti in his hand and laughing uproariously. From these visuals to the song 'Awāra hoon' is yet another smooth transition. This placing of the song explains to a considerable extent the stupendous popularity of the song.

After the heroes of Greek tragedy and the eighteenth/nineteenth century romantic heroes with their different sorrows, there comes the hero of the industrial age, who might not be able to 'do' anything about his sorrows and evils but can at least laugh at them, as he can laugh at himself and laugh at everything in sight, even at the pretty girl he is going to fall in love with. The transition from melodrama to farce is thus heralded by a laughter. We could be even a little more poetic on the theme, but what stands out only too clearly is that while the transitional sound for the childhood sequence had been the traumatic cry of the new-born infant, that for the adulthood sequence is the laughter filled with sarcasm and a devil-may-care attitude.

The film begins in the courtroom, goes back to the killing of Jugga, and then once more returns to the courtroom. Though the FB is not over, the end is approaching. With the repetition of this space/location, the film will begin to flow into the present time, instead of the more usual precise return point. The director once again shows marks of his mature craftsmanship. We are taken back to a point before the FB (as a reminder of the closing of it) by the question from the judge, presiding over the case, 'Who is going to defend the culprit?' The answer from Rita is the same, 'I will fight the case.' But this time she is saying it to Leela. Thus the FB begins to phase out, and comes to an end only when Raj gives up the attempt to kill Raghunath and is naturally caught (a detail not shown).

Another design that can be perceived here centres on the fact that both the fathers, one natural and the other surrogate, are present just before the introduction of the FB, the second transition and the two phasing-out or mingling points. Raghunath, of course, is there at all the important points. The childhood section begins in a conflict with the father, which is in a sense pre-natal, a given conflict; Raj is born with a parental opposition. Jugga's arrival at his birth is that other evil dark shadow on his life. The return to the present time again is marked by the conflict (or end of conflict) with Jugga and then Raghunath in that order.

Seen from the structural point of view, the appearance of Jugga, which seems to be a horrible piece of coincidence, can now be seen in a different light. Whether one takes the heredity-environment question seriously or not is a different matter; but if one recognizes that to be a major thematic preoccupation then one would see that in *Awāra* the theme is not just injected through occasional snatches of dialogue or a couple of dramatic incidents, but is made part of the structural organization of the film.

The last point about the FB factor is that the present time bracketing the past endows the narrative structure with a circularity. Nearly five-eighths of the film is in the past. The circularity suggests a generalization, viz., things will happen the same way always; in other words, it suggests continuity. This much is verbalized again in the courtroom sequence. The long speech by Raj, which does seem somewhat forced and may be even too long, is part of a convention that Kapoor relishes and uses again with greater favour in his next film, *Shree 420;* the speech is justified by its structuring.[1] The other elements that go to underscore the continuity include the boy in the title cards. The boy is not the child Raj. He is any boy—or may be all the boys who are brought up in the slums. The speech in the courtroom draws in visually a group of urchins crowded in the visitors' gallery as the living presence of the generation threatened by the power and authority of Raghunath. The children at this point are an extension/elaboration/culmination of the child in the title cards. The film opens and closes with the image of Raghunath. He is not forgiven for his sins yet his is the world that Raj wants to inhabit. Thus, the rebellion of youth becomes a part of the theme of continuity—of history.

The popular appeal of the film drew from the fact that it is not a tale of youthful rebellion alone or a tale of love which is the modus operandi of the youth, but a parable of rebellion and failure, each rising from and getting incorporated into the other.

This structuring of the film has been worked towards an end where the image of the successful hero and that of the failed hero will be difficult to distinguish; just as it will be difficult to see authority entirely vindicated in Raghunath. This is something that Kapoor has been trying to say in all his films, but it gets said the best in *Awāra*.

A study of the narrative structure helps us to identify the various sections, scenes, sequences or shots and bring to our notice a very crucial aspect of the film— its fragmented nature and the various film styles and conventions attached to different scenes, sequences, etc. Expressionistic composition and lighting, Soviet composition or editing style, the Chaplinesque, Italian neo-realism, Dickensian realism, Hollywood gangster or the film-noir, use of symbolism or kitsch—we find them all in various grades of authenticity or dilution. It will be a stupendous task to identify their individual use in this film or in the history of Indian popular cinema, and study how they have been internalized or subverted.

RAJ KAPOOR—THE
HERO—THE MAN

At the end of the book we finally confront the hero
and the filmmaker, the filmmaker and his film or more
accurately the triptych—character–actor–director—
and the film *Awāra;* in other words, now we have
a tetrad that we will be confronting all at once. We
have gone through the study of the other characters,
we have gone through some of the features of popular
cinema, some of the problematic around it, vis-à-vis
popular cinema in general as well as this film in
particular. All that we have said about and around
the film so far has really gone to define the tetrad in
terms of both cause and effect. There would have been
no point earlier in devoting a chapter to Raj, as hero,
for the entire business of popular cinema—its making,
viewing, etc.—is devoted to the construction of a hero
(or for that matter, a heroine in the melodrama or the
woman-centred film, constructed in terms of a male
director's point of view directed at the woman). When

161

the director of the film acts as the hero, when he also
produces the film, puts in the money for it, writes the
script along with the script-writer, assists in the music
direction, is present during the editing stage, then the
discussion around the film assumes other dimensions.
And we come to discuss him in all his 'roles' together
with the film, at a culminating point of all discussions
and observations.

The hero, as we realize, is not created by the
demands of the story alone; he is created by all the
demands made by and on the medium and by its
history in a particular country. *Awāra* is an interesting
film to watch for Kapoor is so very conscious of what
he is doing, of the medium, of the question of money
revolving around it, of himself as a man and an artist,
and as a performer, who has a close relationship with his
audience. His close association with both cinema and
theatre, his awareness of the contemporary ideology-
based cultural activities of the IPTA and his desire to
find a place in the money-based film industry bring to
his work a density coupled with his tremendous social
charisma.

Kapoor has been described as one of the greatest
of showmen of India. He is a passionate performer
who took full advantage of the performative and
the participatory nature of Indian cinema. As a true
performer he is tremendously interested in the craft of
his medium. If one can look beyond the fragmented
surface of the film, one sees how he has imbibed from

so many sources and has thought of new cinematic expressions. Consequently the film (or all his films) become(s) all the more interesting and enjoyable: do we need to remind ourselves again that what is enjoyable is also interesting and worth verbalization?

When one is talking of an artwork (popular or élite) all the three arms of the famous triangle—artwork–artist–society—are to be taken into account. How can we bring in the (dement of pleasure (or entertainment) to stand between its relationship with the individual thinking coming from its creator and the collective thinking that is shaping it, coming out of its relationship with society? Is it not more interesting to see how an artwork becomes richer because of its relationship with the other two? We have seen how conscious Kapoor was of this factor. The purpose of this book has been to identify in him and some other popular filmmakers the marks of this consciousness. A qualitative analysis of this 'consciousness' and whether or not this was realized could be a topic for other books. This book could only touch upon some points. Of course, it is also to be borne in mind that film talk is, because of that triangular relationship, a very precarious balancing act, and no one approach is ever fully satisfying. It is more so when its status is an indeterminate. And we have observed that too. Not only theatre but cinema too is, in the mind of the makers and the audience, 'the workshop of the devil' as Kewal says in *Aag*. Kapoor's own ambivalent attitude is interesting in the way it has shaped and coloured his films. That which is born out of ambivalence could be treated with an ambivalence of attitude—yes, that is possible. Hence, this entire seriousness of approach does not totally do away with the other non-serious approach.

Popular cinema, because of its intense consumeristic nature, has become a matter of a too fast rate of growth and change—and it does not fulfil a very big prerequisite of art: its staying power. Again, on the other hand, *Awāra* and the other films have proved to have that 'permanency' in the midst of society. The recent trend of looking back at the films of the past with seriousness—as they are being continuously having re-runs or being seen on video—has invested these films with a new status. So we leave one set of problematic attached to popular cinema, to look at another.

Kapoor would like to raise his art to 'transcendental heights', is agonized that his Nataraj and Trimurti Shiv is toppling down; is aware that he must compromise and join hands with the present order and is incapable of starting a 'future order', which he and Abbas wanted Raj to represent. We have discussed what all these mean within the given parameters. Raj–Raj Kapoor–Kapoor—charmers all—all of them one person really, whose films has/have charmed generations of viewers. All this charm is not so fragile that it should crumble if seen in its social and historical perspective.

A star is a mythical being, the making of a star is a mysterious process; it can be a crafted, well-preserved 'lie'. Just as pleasure alone cannot be the reason for taking cinema seriously, similarly lie cannot be the only reason for neglecting it. A so-called serious approach cannot kill pleasure—on the contrary it can even add to the pleasure. Just as one need neither be puritanical nor judgmental about pleasure; nor should pleasure become mindless, heartless excitant, transient and fleeting. It definitely is not so for a society, if we consider it in terms of its production and distribution. It is not easy to talk about a kitsch that 'works' (or hence about one that does not); it will be even more difficult to talk about 'an inspired kitsch'. The popular cinema as an industrial art, as a patchwork art, Indian popular cinema as a mix of Hollywood and Indian folk traditions, etc., are topics that have already invited some amount of attention, in this country and in the West in particular. But like all other traditions of creation or performance it requires a certain a priori acceptance, a condition of belonging within that tradition. Only 'outside criticism' cannot work. Kapoor is also doing that. He works entirely within the tradition, at the same time provides an internal critique. He knows that cinema can be something else, a real tool for protest, a vehicle that truly carries the marks of change (changes that are taking place within the society). His passion rises partly out of that.

We have noted the intense 'individualism' of *Awāra* and its place among other individualistic

films. Because of his multiple role in the process of
filmmaking, Kapoor manages to put into his work
many of his own thoughts, doubts, and passions. Till
Mera Naam Joker, his films are a blend of personal
statements, humour and emotional outbursts, with an
element of unabashed sexuality, sometimes intense and
celebratory and sometimes puritanically confessional.
There are references *to* his personal life, or sometimes
to the showbiz world that make the references appear
as personal history. All that is part of the creation of
the 'actor as the text'. But there comes a time in his
life when this way fails. V.P. Sathe notes, 'Raj Kapoor
made men's films till *MNJ;* when women characters
were entirely passive, reacting but never acting. After
MNJ Raj Kapoor began to make women-centred films
and his male characters then became weak, devoid
of their previous charm and force.' That could be a
fascinating study—to trace the change in his work. But
the strong individualistic hero is not after all so strong:
he is strongly individualistic with an individualism
that erodes a man. Along with the various film styles
and conventions we see Kapoor wearing an array of
'individual' garbs and masks: he is a lover, a thief, an
imprisoned convict, a lover of humanity, a lover of
women, a city-crook, a tragic hero, a tortured soul and
an artist in agony. As a genre-formation principle Raj's–
Raj Kapoor's–Kapoor's individualism is of interest to
us; doubly so because of his awareness of it. He calls
Aag his 'first diary'—he bares himself (as he believes

baring to be.) What gets immediately connected is the issue of audience participation, and together with that the recognition of the various elements of the spectacle in front. We have noted how he fills his films with recognizable little pieces of music, dialogues, etc., from his own other films and others' films as well. What we have then is the study of the popular cinema genre and its dynamics with its audience.

In this process of recognition, identification and participation lies the continuity of a society's being. Popular cinema cannot break a status quo. Popular cinema maintains the status quo and provides a sense of continuity and security for the members of the society who are within its tradition. This requirement arises out of a certain sense of continuity, so crucial to man; a continuity that is forever being jeopardized in a consumeristic world, rapidly growing and changing. Here myths are created and broken with tremendous speed; contemporary history is absorbed immediately and thrown up as reference, quotations or small story elements; that way one is in touch with one's surroundings, immediate history, but without getting a real grasp on it. But the touch cannot be totally lost. Popular art/cinema is always 'in touch' for that alone is its function. (It must be mentioned here that 'audience rejection' of a film, which so baffles filmmakers, is also part of the story of this rapid process.)

The romantic hero in Raj Kapoor is noticed, the Chaplinesque Tramp is noticed, but the violence is not.

Kapoor and the others identified the violence within the medium as the violence of an incomprehensible change. But even the attempts to portray the violence become ultimately diluted, something that Kapoor noted through his story of compromise. Hollywood too has had the phenomenon of the 'violent films' of the fifties or the individualistic films of the forties and the fifties. Perhaps we would have to take note of that history—for some of the waves could have come from those shores. But since the violence is not recognized for what it is, the violence has grown beyond control and confounds the confusion.

The intense discussions today around the questions of voyeurism, the injustice/and violence towards women in the representation of women should give a different dimension to Kapoor's work. For us Kapoor seems to be somewhat aware of the allegorical property behind the representation. All his ambivalence must manifest through it, make it wear whites and blacks, glorify and debase it. I am once again reminded of that sequence in *Aag* where everything is ready for a stage production, but for the *heroine*, Kewal says, 'The heroine is the most important thing in a theatre.' He is upset when he goes through the audition test and bursts out, 'This is not the way one can find a heroine.' What is new is a concern for the various problems associated with a desire for certain excellence. Apart from technical excellence he is also striving for a perfection that is expressed through words such as 'height'—'I want to take theatre to a height'—the reference to theatre is of course a reference to cinema also. The 'height' finds visualization in the dream sequence in *Awāra*. One wishes that Kapoor would delve deeper into this feeling of concern, enquire into what it is that he is really striving for. His concept of 'perfect' and 'imperfect' often finds moral expression in words like 'body' and 'soul' in several of his films. He shows himself as one tormented for perfection, in art and love, and concerned for a 'perfect society'—once again what is lacking is an analysis of these concerns. He seems to be suffering from a constant feeling of lack, which we have already identified as the woe of the modern urban hero, but did not then see it as a feeling of lack for not producing artwork as he would like to have done.

We do not know what Kapoor thought cinema should be but we know the kinds of scrutiny popular cinema is going through today. Literary criticism, cultural anthropology, psychoanalysis and political science are some of the disciplines that, through their independent and multidisciplinary explorations, have thrown up the need for feminist studies. Our film could go through such a scrutiny. I have mentioned why it is not possible yet to do that and have a proper reading of the reason why popular cinema is not 'perfect'. But at least we could study some of the reasons behind its pleasures, its formative principles, and then we will suspend our pleasure to go through other kinds of studies, for which there is need and which will be the subject matter for other works.

NOTES

The Title of the Film

1. An echo from Devdas speaking in P.C. Barua's film *Devdas* (1939), where he says, 'I am what I am not; I am not what I am.' I shall take up this piece of dialogue again in chapter 5.

2. The original story was written by Abbas (1914–87) who had V.P. Sathe for his collaborator when he came to work on the script and the dialogues. The Abbas–Kapoor association continued till *Bobby* (1973) with a break in between; while Sathe continued to write scripts for R.K. Films till *Henna*.

3. Subtitled *The Vagabond* in English, *Awāra* (and Raj Kapoor himself) came to be known as 'Brodigya' or 'Tovarish Brodigya' in Russia.

4. Raj Kapoor had been actually named Ranbir Raj Kapoor by his father, Prithviraj Kapoor, but the women of the family called him Gora after the central character of the novel by Tagore. Two younger brothers born immediately after Raj Kapoor were named Rabindranath and Devendranath. Their early deaths came to affect Raj Kapoor directly.

5. 'The classical Hollywood film typically uses the credits sequence to initiate the film's narration. Even these forty

to ninety seconds cannot be wasted. Furthermore, in these moments, the narration is self-conscious to a high degree. Musical accompaniment already signals the presence of this narration, and often musical motifs in this overture will recur in the film proper'. (David Bordwell, Janet Staiger, Christine Thompson, *The Classical Hollywood Cinema: Film Style and Mode of Production to 1960,* Routledge, London, 1985, p. 25)

The Father, and the Other Generations

1. Right from the outset of the writing of the story, Abbas had conceived Prithviraj Kapoor in the role of the father. When he took the story to Mehboob, the latter suggested Dilip Kumar as the *Awāra* hero, and Abbas (in *I am no Island,* Vikas, New Delhi, 1977, p. 361) records his reaction: 'That would rob the story of the piquancy of the real father and son relationship, which, according to me, was the distinct advantage, a scoop.' Later when he read the story out to Prithviraj, the latter said, 'I suppose you want me to play the hero's old father.' He had only recently played the lead in the bilingual *Rajnartaki* and was a handsome man, hence naturally self-conscious about playing character roles. But I had the answer ready, 'Prithviraj-ji, you are not the hero's father. You are the hero.'

2. Interviewing V.P. Sathe, I began by asking him what in his opinion the film was all about. Sathe's answer was prompt: 'First, there was the old order, i.e., the feudal order; then came the new order, i.e., the capitalistic order. We wanted there to be a third one, and Raj Kapoor was to represent this new order.' I asked him, 'Then why did you show that order failing and Raj left seeking a compromise?' In reply, Sathe just smiled.

3. The choice of the actor K.N. Singh, already 'typed' as a screen villain, to play Jugga, helps in the construction of this sub-text.

The Woman: The Women

1. Malti Sahai and Wimal Dissanayake discuss the aspect of humour in Raj Kapoor's films, in their book *Raj Kapoor's Films: Harmony of Discourse,* Vikas, New Delhi, 1988.
2. The phrase is borrowed from William Elison, 'The Whiteness We Pursue: The Hindi Feature Film under Imperialism', a dissertation submitted at Williams College, 1989.
3. Ann Kaplan, 'Mothering, Feminism and Representation', in Christine Gledhill (ed.), *Home is where the Heart is,* BFI, London, 1987, p. 124.

Love and Romance

1. David Bordwell, in *The Classical Hollywood Cinema,* p. 16.
2. Stanley Cavell, *Pursuits of Happiness: The Hollywood Comedy of Remarriage,* Harvard, 1981, p. 17. Italics mine.
3. The dialogue is borrowed from a short story by Krishenchander, called 'The Night of the Full Moon'.

Genre

1. Stephen Neale, *Genre,* BFI, London, 1980, p. 19.
2. See Iqbal Masud, 'The Fifties. The City: Paradise and Inferno', in *Cinema in India,* NFDC publication, Bombay, July-Sept. 1987, p. 22.

Popularity, Pleasure, Popular Cinema

1. Jane Tompkins, quoted by Christine Gledhill, in 'The Melodramatic Field: An investigation', in *The Home is where the Heart is*.
2. Ashish Rajadhyaksha, 'Neo-Traditionalism: Film as Popular Art in India,' in *Framework*, 32/33, p. 21.
3. S.S. Vasan, 'What is wrong in Indian Cinema', in *Filmfare*.
4. Rajadhyaksha, 'Neo-Traditionalism', p. 22.
5. Mrinal Sen, 'What is a Good Cinema', in *Views on Cinema*, Ishan, Calcutta, 1977, p. 48.
6. Eric Barnouw and S. Krishnaswamy, in their *Indian Film* (Columbia University Press, N.Y., London, 1963, p. 153), give a detailed account of the great popularity that *Awāra* enjoyed all over Asia and in the erstwhile Soviet Union: 'The film had its quota of songs, one of which, "Awāra hoon", swept through Asia. *Awāra* dubbed into Turkish, Persian and Arabic, broke box-office records in the middle-East. Meanwhile in Moscow, where Abbas had won a showing with *Dharti Ke Lai* without causing a furor, *Awāra* swept all before it. The Soviet Union is said to have made a massive distribution of *Awāra* dubbed into a number of its languages. Prints were even flown into Soviet Expeditions near the North Poles. The Soviet distribution began in 1954, after Raj Kapoor, Nargis, Abbas and others had visited Moscow as members of a film delegation. On a return visit to the USSR two years later, Raj Kapoor and Nargis were astonished to find themselves well-known film personalities. Bands played "Awāra hoon" at airports. *Awāra* is reported to have been a favourite film of Mao tse Dzong. It can also be relevant here that in the International Film Festival in 1985 a lot of bitterness and controversy were raised when a Russian film had won the Golden Peacock in Delhi. The film, called *Farewell Green Summer*,

was a tribute to *Awāra* and had some footage of the film. The filmmaker present during the festival spoke of the influence of Raj Kapoor on him when he was young.'

Less widely known is a reference to *Awāra* in Nobel Prize laureate Alexander Solzhenitsyn's *Cancer Ward* (Bantam, New York, 1969, p. 170): 'Suddenly she flung out her arms, snapped the fingers of both hands, her whole body writhing to the urge of the popular song she began singing from a recent Indian film.

"A-va-rai-ya-a-a! A-va-rai-ya-a-a!"

Oleg's face instantly clouded. "No, don't! Not that song, Zoya, please—"

In a flash she assumed an air of strict decorum. No one would have thought that a moment ago she'd been singing and writhing.

"It's from *The Tramp*," she said. "Haven't you seen it?"

"Yes, I have."

"Isn't it a wonderful movie? I saw it twice." (In fact she'd seen it four times, but she didn't quite like to admit it), "Didn't you like it? After all, the tramp's life was rather like yours."

"It wasn't at all!" Oleg frowned. His radiant expression did not return. The warmth of the yellow sun had left him, and it was obvious what a sick man he was after all.

"I mean, he'd just come out of prison too. And his whole life was ruined."

"That was just a bluff. He was a typical grafter, a hood."

Zoya stretched out her hand for her white coat.

Oleg got up, smoothed the coat out and helped her into it.

"I can see you don't like people like that." She nodded her thanks and began to do up her buttons.

"I hate them." He looked past her, a cruel expression on his face. His jaw tightened slightly. It was a disagreeable movement. "They're predators, parasites, they live off other people. For the last thirty years we've had it drummed into us that these people are reforming, that they're now almost our social equals, but they work on the same principle as Hitler: 'If you're not being'—the next word's an obscenity, it's got punch to it, but it really means—If you are not being beaten, sit quiet and wait your turn. If your neighbour's being stripped naked and you are not, sit quiet and wait your turn. They are only too happy to kick a man when he's down, and then they have the nerve to wrap themselves up in a cloak of romanticism, while we help them create a legend, and even their songs are sometimes sung on the screen.'"

Rita and Raghunath: Pursuits of Whiteness/Incest

1. The dinner serves as a metaphor for 'Westernization', through the metonymy (parts for a whole) of the paraphernalia of ceremony, viz., the soup, the soup-spoon, and the 'correct' way of eating soup.
2. In his writing, Ghatak refers to Levi-Strauss, whose *The Elementary Structures of Kinship* (Eyre and Spottiswoode, London, 1969) offers a study of incest.

Music in Awāra

1. Incidentally, the tune is the same as that of a song we sang in schools in West Bengal in our childhood—beginning '*inti binti . . .*'

The Narrative Structure

1. The courtroom speech, a takeoff from Chaplin's Monsieur
   Verdoux speech, is yet another tribute to Chaplin, on whose
   'Tramp' Kapoor modelled several of his impersonations.
   The boy under the gas lamp-post (and the several other
   uses of the gas-lamp itself) carries echoes from Chaplin's
   Easy Street, City Lights, and *The Kid.*